CAST

TIM BARROW | THOMAS
Tim trained at Drama Centre London. Theatre credits include: *Translations* (Citizens Theatre); *The Idiot At The Wall* (Stoirm Òg); *The Killing Moon, The Tin Horizon* (Theatre503); *The Giant Killers* (Long Lane); *Julius Caesar, The Taming of the Shrew, Richard III, Antony and Cleopatra, Henry V, The Tempest, As You Like It* (Bard In The Botanics); *Duchess of Malfi* (Glasgow Repertory Company); *Horizontal Collaboration* (Fire Exit); *Our Boys* (Theatre Enigma); *Romeo and Juliet* (Prime Productions); *A War of Two Halves, It's a Wonderful Life, A Christmas Carol, A Midsummer Night's Dream* (Nonsense Room). Television and film credits include: *Outlander* (Starz); *Taggart* (ITV); *Waterloo Road* (BBC); *New Town Killers; Tomorrow Might Be The Day* (SFTN/Shakehaus); *Guardians* (Braine Hownd Films); *Lucky Star* (SFTN/Hopscotch Films); *The Queen's Wedding* (Mentorn); *Christmas in the Highlands* (Triventure Films); *Children of the Dead End; The Tony Miller Story* (BBC Alba); *Distant Sky; Fertility Daze; The Inheritance, The Space Between, Riptide* (Lyre Films).

MICHAEL DYLAN | NATHAN
Michael Dylan trained at the Guildhall School of Music and Drama, London. His work in theatre includes: *Richard III* (Perth Theatre); *The Lying Kind* (Tron Theatre); *Girl in the Machine* (Traverse Theatre); *White* (Catherine Wheels Theatre Company/Europe and Asia tour); *The Lonesome West* (Tron Theatre/Russian tour); *One Man Two Guvnors* (National Theatre/UK and Ireland tour); *Ulysses* (Tron Theatre/Irish tour); *Mikey and Addie* (Macrobert); *A Midsummer Night's Dream* (Headlong); *Comedians* (Lyric Hammersmith); *Moonshadow* (White Bear, London; Time Out's Critics' Choice); *Black Comedy* (Bridewell Theatre, London); *Deirdre of the Sorrows* (Irish national tour). Television and film credits include: *Shetland, Bert and Dickie* (BBC); *Big Brother – Secrets and Lies* (Endemol); *Muppets Most Wanted* (Disney); *For George* (For George Productions).

MARYAM HAMIDI | NORA 2/CHRISTINE 1
Stage credits include: *Nursery Crymes* (Mischief La Bas); *Hysteria* (Òran Mór); *Flight* (Vox Motus); *Betrayed* (Tron Theatre); *Others* (Paper Birds); *Home: Glasgow, The Recovery Position, Oedipus, Self Contained* (National Theatre of Scotland); *The Chronicles of Irania* (A Moment's Peace); *The Library* (Frozen Charlotte); *The Three Little Pigs* (Platform); *Local Reality Expo* (Clare Duffy/CCA); *Niqabi Ninja* (Platform/Sara Sharawi); *The Algebra of Freedom* (7:84); *When the Lights Went Out* (Tara Arts). Her screen credits include: *Wild Rose* (Fable Pictures/Film4); *Last Night in Edinburgh* (SoCiArts); *Where Do We Go From Here?* (Worrying Drake); *Make Me Up* (Hopscotch/Rachel McLean); *Forest Hills* (UPHA/BBC) and a regular role on BBC Scotland's *River City*, as well as numerous radio plays for BBC Radio most recently, *The Ethical Hacking Bureau, After Fear, The Road To Bani Walid, Providing* and *Birth: Syria*.

ANNA RUSSELL-MARTIN | NORA 1/CHRISTINE 3

Anna trained at The Dance School of Scotland and the Royal Conservatoire of Scotland. She is this year's Citizens Theatre Actor Intern. Theatre credits include: *A Christmas Carol* (Citizens Theatre); *Cyrano de Bergerac* (National Theatre of Scotland/Citizens Theatre/Royal Lyceum Theatre Edinburgh); *Bunny* (Tron Theatre); *The Wonderful World of Dissocia, The Angry Brigade, One More Sleep 'til Christmas, Coriolanus* (Royal Conservatoire of Scotland); *Betty Blue Eyes, Godspell* (The Dance School of Scotland/Citizens Theatre). Awards include: the Duncan MacRae Memorial Award for Scots Language 2016 and the Arnold Fleming Scholarship 2016. Anna was awarded the Mac Brydon Prize 2018.

MOLLY VEVERS | NORA 3/CHRISTINE 2

Molly trained at the Royal Conservatoire of Scotland. Theatre credits include: *Othello* (English Touring Theatre); *Seanmhair* (The Other Room, The Edinburgh Festival Fringe); *Ross & Rachel* (Battersea Arts Centre/59e59 Theaters New York/UK tour); *Jumpy* (Royal Lyceum Theatre Edinburgh); *A First World Problem* (Theatre503); *The Sleeping Beauties* (Sherman Cymru); *Kora* (Magnetic North/Dundee Rep); *Time and the Conways* (Royal Lyceum Theatre Edinburgh/Dundee Rep); *The Snow Queen, She Town* (Dundee Rep). Television and film credits include: *Doctors* (BBC); *Doors Open* (ITV); *Chubby Funny* (Free Range Films/AimImage Productions), *Bittersweet* (BFI Film Academy). Molly won the Stage Award for Acting Excellence 2015 for her performance in *Ross & Rachel*.

DANIEL WARD | DANIEL

Daniel trained at the National Youth Theatre and LAMDA. Theatre credits include: *Hearing Things* (Omnibus Theatre); *A Wake In Progress* (VAULT Festival); *Abigail's Party* (Hull Truck); *Divas* (The Pleasance); *The Barbershop Chronicles* (Fuel Theatre/Òran Mór); *The 24 Hour Plays: Old Vic New Voices* (The Old Vic/The 24 Hour Company); *The Amen Corner* (National Theatre); *Fathers Inside, White Boy* (Soho Theatre); *Measure for Measure* (Liverpool Everyman).

CREATIVE TEAM

STEF SMITH | WRITER

Work includes: *My England* (Young Vic); *Love Letter to Europe* (Underbelly); *Girl in the Machine* and *Swallow* (Traverse Theatre); *Human Animals* (Royal Court); *Remote* (National Theatre Connections Festival); *Tea and Symmetry* (BBC Radio); *Smoke and Mirrors* (Traverse Theatre/DOT Istanbul for Theatre Uncut); *Back to Back to Back* (Cardboard Citizens); *Cured* (Glasgay! Festival); *Grey Matter* (The Lemon Tree); *Falling/Flying* (Tron Theatre). Her critically acclaimed show, *Roadkill*, won numerous awards, including an Olivier Award for Outstanding Achievement in an Affiliate Theatre; *Swallow* won a Scotsman Fringe First Award and Scottish Arts Club Theatre Award. Stef took part in the BBC Drama Writers Room and is currently under commission at the Traverse Theatre, Leeds Playhouse, Headlong and the National Theatre of Scotland. She is also an Associate Artist at the Traverse Theatre and Leeds Playhouse.

ELIZABETH FREESTONE | DIRECTOR

Elizabeth's credits include: *Queen Margaret* (Royal Exchange Theatre, Manchester); *Henry V* (Shakespeare at the Tobacco Factory); *The Rape of Lucrece, Here Lies Mary Spindler, The Tragedy of Thomas Hobbes, The Comedy of Errors* (Royal Shakespeare Company); *Endless Light* (Kali Theatre/Southwark Playhouse); *The Duchess of Malfi, Dr Faustus, The School for Scandal, Volpone* (Greenwich Theatre); *Romeo and Juliet* (Shakespeare's Globe); *The Water Harvest* (Theatre503) and *Left On Church Street* (Bridewell Theatre). She is the former Artistic Director of Pentabus for whom she directed *Here I Belong, From Land to Mouth, As The Crow Flies, The Lone Pine Club, Milked, Each Slow Dusk, In This Place, For Once, Blue Sky* and *Stand Up Diggers All*. Elizabeth was the Associate Director for *People, Places and Things* at St Ann's Warehouse in New York and *A Caucasian Chalk Circle* at the National. She was a Staff Director at the National, the Royal Shakespeare Company, Hampstead Theatre, Soho Theatre and the Royal Court Theatre. She trained at Rose Bruford College and the National Theatre Studio.

TOM PIPER | DESIGNER

Recent designs include: *Hay Fever, King Lear, Hamlet, The Libertine* (Citizens Theatre); *Cyrano de Bergerac* (Citizens Theatre/National Theatre of Scotland/Royal Lyceum Theatre Edinburgh); *Long Day's Journey Into Night, Endgame* (Citizens Theatre/HOME Manchester); *Rhinoceros* (Royal Lyceum Theatre Edinburgh); *The Great Wave* (National Theatre); *The Cherry Orchard* (Bristol Old Vic/Royal Exchange Theatre, Manchester); *iHo* (Hampstead Theatre); *Harrogate* (HighTide/Royal Court Theatre); *A Midsummer Night's Dream, Romeo and Juliet* (Royal Shakespeare Company/UK tour); *Carmen La Cubana* (Le Théâtre du Châtelet); *Red Velvet* (West End/Tricycle Theatre/New York); *White Teeth* (Kiln Theatre); *The King's Speech* (Birmingham Rep/Chichester Festival

Theatre/UK tour); *Orfeo* (Royal Opera House); *Tamburlaine the Great* (Theatre For a New Audience, New York/Royal Shakespeare Company). As Associate Designer of the Royal Shakespeare Company, Tom designed over 45 of their shows including *The Histories* for which he won an Olivier for Best Costume Design. Tom designed *Blood Swept Lands and Seas of Red* at the Tower of London and received an MBE for services to Theatre and First World War commemorations. Other recent exhibitions include: *Winnie-the-Pooh: Exploring a Classic* (V&A); *Shakespeare Staging The World* (British Museum); *Beyond the Deepening Shadows* (Flame installation at the Tower of London).

LEE CURRAN | LIGHTING DESIGNER
Theatre includes: *Summer and Smoke* (Almeida Theatre/Duke of York's Theatre); *Jesus Christ Superstar* (Regent's Park Open Air Theatre/Lyric Opera Chicago); *Constellations* (Royal Court/Duke of York's Theatre/ Broadway/UK tour); *Gundog, Road, Nuclear War, a profoundly affectionate, passionate devotion to someone (–noun), X, Linda* (Royal Court Theatre); *Berberian Sound Studio, The Lady from the Sea, Splendour* (Donmar Warehouse); *Dance Nation* (Almeida Theatre); *The Son* (Kiln Theatre); *Jubilee* (Royal Exchange Theatre, Manchester/Lyric Hammersmith); *Woyzeck* (Birmingham Rep); *A Streetcar Named Desire, The Weir* (English Touring Theatre); *Black Men Walking* (Eclipse Theatre/ UK tour), *Burgerz* (Hackney Showroom); *Doctor Faustus* (Royal Shakespeare Company); *The Winter's Tale* (Royal Lyceum Theatre Edinburgh); *Imogen* (Shakespeare's Globe); *Depart* (LIFT); *Kissing The Shotgun Goodnight* (Christopher Brett Bailey); *A Number* (Young Vic/Nuffield Theatre); *Mametz* (National Theatre Wales); *Protest Song* (National Theatre). Dance includes: *Blak Whyte Gray* (Boy Blue Entertainment); *Grey Matter, E2 7SD* (Rambert2); *Tomorrow, Frames, Curious Conscience* (Rambert); *Sun, Political Mother, In Your Rooms, The Art of Not Looking Back, Uprising* (Hofesh Shechter). Opera includes: *Orphee Et Eurydice* (Royal Opera House/Teatro Alla Scala); *Tosca* (Opera North).

MICHAEL JOHN MCCARTHY | COMPOSER / SOUND DESIGNER
Michael John is a Cork-born, Glasgow-based composer, musician and sound designer. Work for performance includes: *Trainspotting, The Gorbals Vampire, Rapunzel, Into That Darkness, Fever Dream: Southside, Sports Day* (Citizens Theatre); *Wendy and Peter Pan, The Hour We Knew Nothing of Each Other, Glory on Earth, A Number, The Weir, Bondagers* (Royal Lyceum Theatre Edinburgh); *What Girls Are Made Of, Ulster American, Gut, How To Disappear, Grain In The Blood* (Traverse Theatre); *Pride & Prejudice* (*Sort Of*) (Tron Theatre/Blood of the Young); *God of Carnage, The Lonesome West, Under Milk Wood* (Tron Theatre); *Jimmy's Hall* (Abbey Theatre); *Rocket Post, In Time O' Strife, The Tin Forest, The Day I Swapped My Dad for Two Goldfish* (National Theatre of Scotland); *August: Osage County, George's Marvellous Medicine, The Cheviot, The Stag and The Black, Black Oil, The BFG, Steel Magnolias* (Dundee Rep); *Light Boxes, Letters Home, The Authorised Kate Bane* (Grid Iron).

EMILY-JANE BOYLE | MOVEMENT DIRECTOR

EJ is a choreographer and movement director, and Artistic Associate of Dundee Rep Theatre. Theatre work includes: *Trainspotting, Cuttin' A Rug* (Citizens Theatre); *Oresteia: This Restless House, Lanark: A Life in Three Acts* (Citizens Theatre/Edinburgh International Festival); *Exit The King* (National Theatre); *The Cheviot, the Stag and the Black Black Oil, Great Expectations, Much Ado About Nothing, Victoria, Snow Queen* (Dundee Rep); *Sunshine on Leith, Richard III* (Leeds Playhouse); *The Red Balloon* (National Youth Ballet); *Pride and Prejudice* (*Sort Of)* (Tron Theatre/ Blood of the Young); *Still Game: Live* (Glasgow Hydro); *Forest Boy* (Noisemaker/NYMF/Arcola Theatre); *Hedda Gabler, The Lion the Witch and the Wardrobe, Jumpy* (Royal Lyceum Theatre Edinburgh); *The Return, Not About Heroes* (Eden Court). Screen work includes: *The Crown* (Netflix); *In Plain Sight* (ITV); *Two Doors Down* (BBC); *God Help the Girl* (Barry Mendel). Other work: Creative Associate/Choreographer *Glasgow 2014 Commonwealth Games;* Assistant Artistic Director *Baku 2015 European Games;* Associate Director *Out of This World* (Sadler's Wells).

RAYMOND SHORT | FIGHT DIRECTOR

Raymond started choreographing fights for his local Karate club at the age of 12. He graduated from Royal Conservatoire of Scotland (formerly RSAMD) in 1994 and is now Combat Lecturer and Fight Director for the company. He has choreographed and directed fights all over the UK and abroad, and worked for companies including Citizens Theatre, National Theatre of Scotland, Scottish Opera, Tron Theatre, Royal Lyceum Theatre Edinburgh, Traverse Theatre, Pitlochry Festival Theatre, Dundee Rep, Perth Rep, Eden Court, Visible Fictions, Catherine Wheels, Babel Theatre, Royal Court Liverpool and The Courtyard. He has also worked for many other touring companies, youth theatres, colleges and community groups, as well as on screen for the BBC, STV and several independent film companies.

JOANNA BOWMAN | ASSISTANT DIRECTOR

Joanna is currently on placement at the Citizens Theatre as part of her MFA in Theatre Directing at Birkbeck, University of London. During her placement Joanna has worked as assistant director on *A Christmas Carol, Cyrano de Bergerac* and *The Macbeths*. Previous credits include: *Delay Detach* (Edinburgh Festival Fringe; Runner Up Scottish Arts Club Theatre Award); *Hedda Gabler* (Byre Theatre).

CITIZENS THEATRE

'As theatrical icons go, few come bigger than Glasgow's Citizens Theatre' *The Herald*

The Citizens Theatre is Glasgow's major producing theatre and one of the leading theatre companies in the UK. Over the last 75 years, we have built an international reputation for producing innovative shows on stage, alongside a highly regarded learning programme of participatory and education work. Led by Artistic Director, Dominic Hill who is regarded as having 'a talent for classical drama which is genuinely world class' (*Daily Telegraph*) we present bold new interpretations of classic texts that are accessible and relevant – and uniquely, where any member of our audience can attend a performance for as little as 50p.

We believe in breaking down barriers to engagement with the arts and that everyone should have the opportunity to take part. Throughout the year we offer a range of opportunities for people of all ages and backgrounds to get involved in the creative life of our theatre.

Our beautiful Victorian home in the Gorbals is currently closed while it undergoes a major redevelopment. This will be the first comprehensive, integrated redevelopment of the building in its 140-year history. It will ensure the Citizens is accessible to all audiences, artists, participants and the local community for generations to come. During the project, our shows are being presented at Tramway and across Scotland, with classes and activities based at Scotland Street School Museum.

For the latest information about the Citizens Theatre visit **citz.co.uk**

Citizens Theatre, 119 Gorbals Street, Glasgow, G5 9DS
Box Office: 0141 429 0022 | Admin: 0141 429 5561

Citizens Theatre Ltd. Registered No. SC022513 and is a Scottish Charity No. SC001337

NORA : A DOLL'S HOUSE

Stef Smith

After Henrik Ibsen

Acknowledgements

My sincere appreciation to the cast, crew and creatives who were involved in the premiere production of *Nora : A Doll's House*. And of course, to the brilliant team at the Citizens Theatre.

My thanks to Dominic Hill for developing and believing in this play, Frances Poet for her endless support, and as always my agent Davina Shah and the team at MLR.

With thanks to my friends who held me up during the making of this play. Especially, Dawn & Ewan, Rose & Jack and Helen & Alan – who without question gave me their homes and hearts. And my family for their endless encouragement, support and stories of the 1980s.

Finally, thank you to Elizabeth Freestone for her care, courage and collaboration.

S.S.

sometimes
the whole world of women
seems a landscape of
red blood and things
that need healing,
the fears all
fears of the flesh;
will it open
or close
will it scar or
keep bleeding
will it live
will it live
will it live and
will he murder it or
marry it.

Lucille Clifton
'she is dreaming'

In a murderous time
            the heart breaks and breaks
                        and lives by breaking.
It is necessary to go
            through dark and deeper
                        dark and not to turn.

Stanley Kunitz
'The Testing-Tree'

Characters

NORA 1
NORA 2
NORA 3
THOMAS 1
THOMAS 2
THOMAS 3
CHRISTINE 1
CHRISTINE 2
CHRISTINE 3
NATHAN 1
NATHAN 2
NATHAN 3
DANIEL 1
DANIEL 2
DANIEL 3

For the premiere production in the spring of 2019, we used the following doubling:

NORA 1/CHRISTINE 3
NORA 2/CHRISTINE 1
NORA 3/CHRISTINE 2

When the script states NORA *(all), all the performers playing Nora should perform those words.*

THOMAS 1/2/3
NATHAN 1/2/3
DANIEL 1/2/3

When the script states THOMAS *(all), all the performers* not *playing Nora should perform those words.*

Writer's Note

Any character with a '1' after their name exists in 2018

Any character with a '2' after their name exists in 1968

Any character with a '3' after their name exists in 1918

This play is set in a living room, over three consecutive days in December.

The writer suggests that on stage there are two doors – one leading to the outside world, one leading into the rest of the house. There should be some chairs for people to sit on, there might also be a Christmas tree.

For simplicity and clarity all stage directions refer to the singular, i.e. 'Nora', not 'Noras'. This does not mean the action should not / cannot be performed by all the performers.

A forward slash (/) denotes an interruption.

Where entirely necessary the actors can change words to suit their own dialect.

All and any suggestions to the set, design, movement, entrances and exits are meant merely as helpful guidance. Imagine it as you wish.

This text went to press before the end of rehearsals and so may differ slightly from the play as performed.

DAY ONE

NORA 1   A woman walks into her home. It's warm
and welcoming, unlike outside where there
is ice on the ground and snow in the air and
not far from here a river has slowed down to
a standstill. The woman enters her home
and her hands and heart thaw. She enters her
home and her breath changes from a ghostly
swirl to being unnoticeable. She enters her
home and there is a particular smell that hits
the back of her throat, lavender. A scent that
covers the smell of carpets and children and
milk and medicine and sweat and sick and
shit and sex and sin and... lavender. Years
ago, she decided she wanted her whole life
to smell of lavender and so, it does. The
smell helps keep her calm as she drags in
the Christmas tree. It's a little sad looking,
a little sullen looking. She haggled the man
down to half-price and then gave him a
touch more as a tip. Even though she
shouldn't have, even though she doesn't
have it to spend on a tip, she did. Kindness
comes back around, she thought as she
dragged the dead-looking spruce through
the streets. She dragged it across six
crossings with a stack of shopping bags
slung over her shoulder and a smile on her
face. And the whole time she hummed in a
note slightly too high for her voice, so that
by the time she was home her throat was
burning. Though she quite liked that feeling
of fire happening inside of her. It kept her
going as she dragged the crumbling

	Christmas tree up the stairs to her house. Bump. Bump. Bump /
NORA 2	A woman walks into her home. It's warm and welcoming, unlike outside where there is ice on the ground and snow in the air and not far from here a river has slowed down to a standstill. The woman enters her /
NORA 3	A woman walks into her home. It's warm and welcoming, unlike outside where there is ice on the ground and snow in the air and not far from here a river has slowed down to a /
NORA 2	A woman walks into her home. It's warm and welcoming /
NORA 1	Unlike outside where there is ice /
NORA 3	On the ground and snow in the /
NORA 1	Lavender. Years ago, she decided she wanted her whole life to smell of /
NORA 2	Carpets and children and milk and medicine and /
NORA 3	A crumbling Christmas tree /
NORA 2	A pocket of pills /
NORA 3	A bag of sugar /
NORA 1	A bottle of /
NORA 2	She passed her children playing and she pretended not to notice.
NORA 3	She passed her children playing and their laughs were /
NORA 1	Bump. Bump. Bump /
NORA 2	She passed her children playing and /
NORA 1	She passed her children playing and /

NORA 3	The burning inside of her.
NORA 2	That feeling of fire.
NORA 1	A smile on her face.
NORA 2	She thinks of holding her children. That very particular way you hold a child.
NORA 3	That very particular way her husband holds her.
NORA 1	She thinks of holding her children /
NORA 2	She thinks of how her husband holds her /
NORA 3	Panting and praying and sweating and /
NORA 2	Bump. Bump. Bump /
NORA 1	Lavender and lovely /
NORA 3	And sweating and swearing and /
NORA 2	Lovely and loving /
NORA 3	And panting and /
NORA 1	Fuck. She expels on an exhale.

NORA *catches her breath. Studies the tree. Takes off her jacket.*

Fuck.

A moment of silence.

NORA 3	And these three different and distinct lives ripple out and grip and grope at the seams of the other's existence.
NORA 2	Three different and distinct women stand on the edge of each

other's /

NORA 3	A woman stands /
NORA 1	The women stand beside their bags of shopping. And sigh.

NORA *sighs*.

NORA 3	Because it's 1918.
NORA 2	It's 1968.
NORA 1	It's 2018.
NORA 3	And out of her handbag she pulls a bag of sugar.
NORA 2	A little case of pills.
NORA 1	A small bottle of alcohol.
NORA 3	Rations had restricted her diet, so, no matter how much money she had to spend she was only given a single small bag of sugar, and she does have money to spend. Well, her husband has money to spend.
NORA 2	And she might not have too much of anything, but she has plenty of these powdery unpleasant-tasting pills. These little helpers of middle-class mothers.
NORA 1	And it's one of those small bottles of alcohol, that people only buy when they are broke or broken or both. She could only afford a small one because her purse holds only air and anxiety.
NORA 3	She unravels the top of the bag, licks a digit and dips it in. And she places that sugar-covered finger in her mouth where the taste of sweetness and sin allows her to escape. Just for a second.
NORA 2	She'd been taking the pills for a few months and when one didn't work, she took two and now, on the cusp of Christmas, she takes three. And as she places them on her tongue and swallows, the relief comes towards her like a liferaft.

NORA 1	She unscrews the top and takes a swig straight out the bottle. A little rush of rock and roll in amongst the managing and mothering. A little rush of rebellion.
THOMAS (*all*)	(*Offstage.*) Nora?
NORA (*all*)	Yes?
THOMAS 1	(*Offstage.*) Nora?
NORA 1	What?
	THOMAS *enters*.
THOMAS 1	You took your time.
NORA 1	Town was hectic.
THOMAS 1	I sent the kids to play next door.
NORA 1	I saw. They're out in her garden, you should have given them gloves.
THOMAS 1	They were driving me up the wall.
NORA 1	It's Christmas, what do you expect?
	THOMAS *looks at the tree*.
THOMAS 1	Is that the tree from last year?
NORA 1	It's nothing decorations won't fix.
THOMAS 1	Miracle-worker, are you?
NORA 1	It's got character.
THOMAS 1	That's just a nice way of saying it's fucking ugly.
NORA 1	It was half-price being so close to Christmas and everything.
THOMAS 1	Half-price? They should have paid you to take it away.
NORA 1	You'll need to get the decorations down from the cupboard. I can't reach them.

And don't look at me like that – I thought it would be nice to get a real tree.

THOMAS 1   Clearly.

NORA 1   Come on. Don't you think we should celebrate? I mean how many men on this street can say they've got a new job?

THOMAS 1   I don't start until January.

NORA 1   But how many can say they've got a brand-new job – starting in January. A brand-new – manager's job. How many men? None. And that's a fact. Though you'll need to start ironing your shirts. Which reminds me – let me show you where the iron is kept.

THOMAS 1   Isn't the ironing your job?

NORA 1   I tell you what, I'll iron your shirts, if you start hoovering or doing the dishes or making the kids' packed lunches or cleaning the bathroom or mopping the floors. Do you even know where we keep the bleach?

THOMAS 1   Yeah. It's... by the iron.

She shoots him a look.

Alright. I'll iron my own shirts.

NORA *moves close to* THOMAS.

NORA 1   But you know I am proud of you. You worked hard for that job. A few years ago, it would have been impossible for you, for us. But it seems like even in this shitty corner of the city, miracles are possible.

THOMAS 1   Oh, I know miracles are possible. Because I found you.

THOMAS *puts his hands around* NORA, *she pushes him off.*

NORA 1	You're such a sap. But I do think we should celebrate. Just… a little.
THOMAS 1	A little? I didn't know you even knew those words.
NORA 1	What's that meant to mean?
THOMAS 1	I know you. You're a little magpie.
NORA 1	You mean common?
THOMAS 1	No. You are anything but common. You are… a skylark.
NORA 1	And what's a skylark?
THOMAS 1	It's stunning. There are loads of them up north in the summer. It's meant to have one of the most beautiful… songs. A songbird.

He puts his arms around her.

You're my little songbird.

They kiss. THOMAS *spots all her shopping bags.*

And what is all this?

NORA 1	Nothing you need to know about.
THOMAS 1	Even though my money bought it? What is this /
NORA 1	No! That is a surprise.
THOMAS 1	For me?
NORA 1	Maybe.
THOMAS 1	Nora.
NORA 1	What?
THOMAS 1	You know what. All this – shit.
NORA 1	It's just a few things.

THOMAS 1	Just a few things?
NORA 1	I like /
THOMAS 1	Spending?
NORA 1	I just like /
THOMAS 1	Stuff. You like having stuff. I go through your pockets and you know what I find? Scratchcards. Like you're collecting them. Scratchcards and Lottery tickets. You're silly believing that /
NORA 1	You shouldn't go through my pockets.
THOMAS 1	And you shouldn't spend all our money, or didn't you notice all those red letters? You need to learn to keep yourself on the ground. Because half of this stuff is on your credit card, isn't it?

NORA *doesn't answer.*

And you know I hate that. I hate the borrowing and the scrabbling and the search for cash because if we're not careful... I just want us to be careful.

NORA 1	And I just want us to have a nice Christmas. For the first time in... I just want to us to have a nice Christmas.

For the kids.

Silence.

THOMAS 1	Okay. Alright.

THOMAS *goes into his pocket. Pulls out money and puts it in front of* NORA. *She goes to take it, he pulls it away from her before she get it. He laughs.*

That's not for spending on me or you. That's for the kids.

NORA 1	Gotcha. And thank you.
THOMAS 1	Shouldn't I get a kiss for that?
	NORA hesitates, kisses him on the cheek.
	And I suppose I should check what is it you want for Christmas or is that a secret too?
NORA 1	Oh. It's no secret. Just a little something... whatever you think you can... give.
THOMAS 1	Money isn't much of a gift.
NORA 1	Then I'll wrap it up in gold paper and hang it off the tree.
	She breathes on his neck. Almost kissing his lips. Teases him.
THOMAS 1	You've lies in the whites of your eyes, Nora. What have you done?
NORA 1	The only thing I've done is turn you on.
	NORA goes to walk away, THOMAS grabs her.
THOMAS 1	You know I can smell booze on your breath?
NORA 1	So, what?
THOMAS 1	So, sing for me. My little songbird.
	THOMAS kisses her. They stop kissing. She tries to pull away, but he holds on to her.
NORA 1	The kids could walk in.
THOMAS 1	I'll put the lock on.
NORA 1	But what if they /
THOMAS 1	Just relax.
	She tries to pull away, but he holds on to her.
NORA 1	I don't think it's /

THOMAS 1	I said just relax.
NORA 1	No, but /
THOMAS 1	Nora!
	NORA *pushes* THOMAS *away.*
NORA 1	We'll – later? Alright?
NORA 3	And she thinks of how her skin used to burn with his touch.
NORA 1	Of how he used to be all she wanted.
NORA 2	Of how much he wants her.
THOMAS 1	I am just trying to make you feel nice.
NORA 1	But don't you have some Christmas decorations to get?
THOMAS 1	But don't you want to fuck?
	Silence.
NORA 1	You're not meant to talk to me like that.
THOMAS 1	Fucking hell. These days it feels like there are more wrong things to say than right. You've been reading too many magazines with all those angry women in them. And stop worrying, will you? This year won't be like... I'm better now. Christmas will be fine.
NORA (*all*)	No. Christmas will be perfect.
	THOMAS *turns to leave.*
THOMAS 1	And by the way – you look beautiful in this light. Something how your hair just... you're lovely.
NORA (*all*)	Thank you.
	THOMAS *leaves.* NORA *watches him.*

NORA 1	And she stands in her living room surrounded by presents, she thinks of her husband's new employment.
NORA 3	As Director of the Bank.
NORA 2	As Head of Credit and Collections.
NORA 1	As Manager of a Short-Term Lender.
NORA 3	And for the first time in years she feels hope.
NORA 2	And as the feeling falls across her face, for a moment she becomes someone else, entirely.
NORA 3	Just for a blink.
NORA 1	She reveals the woman underneath.

A knock at the door.

Kids. I told you not to do that.

She opens it.

Oh. Sorry I thought you were...

CHRISTINE 1	Nora? Is that you? Nora Helmer? That is your married name isn't it? Am I saying it right?
NORA 1	Yeah?
CHRISTINE 1	You don't remember me? Do you?
NORA 1	I'm sorry I...
CHRISTINE 1	In all fairness, it's been – what – nearly ten years?
NORA 1	No, I.... No. Can't be.
CHRISTINE 1	Am I that different?
NORA 1	Christine!?
CHRISTINE 1	Nora!

NORA 1   Oh my god... Christine. You've... you've
                  changed... you've... what am I doing –
                  you're here! Come in. Come in from the
                  cold. Take off your jacket. Warm up it's
                  so... cold.

                  CHRISTINE *enters the living room.*

                  Now I see. I see – you. But you've lost
                  weight? You're half the girl /

CHRISTINE 1   I'm not a girl, Nora. I'm older, we both are.

NORA 1   Just a little older. Maybe. Just a tiny bit.

CHRISTINE 1   I know you shouldn't turn up without asking
                  but I thought it would be fun for my visit to
                  be a surprise – so, surprise!

                  She takes off her jacket. NORA *stares at
                  her. Silence.*

                  You're quiet.

NORA 1   I'm sorry. It's just a shock. I suddenly feel
                  a hundred years old.

CHRISTINE 1   Well, you don't look it. Barely look a day
                  older. Are those kids out there yours?

NORA 1   Yeah.

CHRISTINE 1   Fucking hell. Three?

NORA 1   Yeah.

CHRISTINE 1   Fucking hell.

NORA 1   Yeah. You've kids?

CHRISTINE 1   God, no. I killed a cactus last week – which
                  I didn't know was even possible. I'm fancy-
                  free and loving it.

NORA 1   Loving it?

CHRISTINE 1   Why wouldn't I be?

NORA 1	Yeah, course. A drink? A coffee? A tea? A whisky? Anything – I can't stand someone with empty hands.
CHRISTINE 1	No, I'm fine.
NORA 1	Are you hungry? I haven't got much in, but I can make some /
CHRISTINE 1	No, I'm fine.
NORA 1	A glass of water?
CHRISTINE 1	I'm fine.
NORA 1	Are you sure? I might even have some /
CHRISTINE 1	It's okay. Don't fuss. No need to do a single thing. Just sit with me... I want to see you. Just you.
	Silence.
NORA 1	Let me get you that glass of water.
	NORA *exits.* CHRISTINE *enters.*
CHRISTINE 2	I like your kitchen, Nora. It's very... yellow. I mean that wallpaper is certainly... something.
NORA 2	It's a little old-fashioned but Tom likes it that way. Are you sure I can't get you a drink, Christine? A festive tipple?
CHRISTINE 2	It's a little too early for a whisky lemonade – do you still drink them?
NORA 2	I've been known to.
CHRISTINE 2	Good. I really hope you haven't changed a bit, Nora. You were always so – lovely.
NORA 2	I suppose I may have changed a little, Christine. As you said, we are no longer girls.

CHRISTINE 2	But what fun we used to have – all those boys that used to chase after you. All those boys I used to chase after...
NORA 2	When was it I last saw you?
CHRISTINE 2	It was the year my mother died. I remember it. You came to her funeral wearing this bright-red lipstick.
NORA 2	Well, that sounds totally inappropriate.
CHRISTINE 2	No, it was beautiful. You looked... so, that would have been 1960.
NORA 2	So, it has been eight years.
CHRISTINE 2	In a blink half a century will have passed. I'm sure of it. So, you must tell me – everything. Tell me happy stories, your stories were always filled with such happiness.
NORA 2	Well, I have a husband – Thomas, Tom and the three children. You will have passed them as you walked here. You've children?
CHRISTINE 2	Me? God, no. I had a man, but... tell me about your Tom.
NORA 2	Well. He is about to start a new job – in a bank. He looks after those new credit cards, have you seen them? Little miracles, really.
CHRISTINE 2	Yeah. I've heard about them. Very modern.
NORA 2	And I'm very proud of him. He worked, well, he worked very hard for it – had to do all these courses and whatnot. I can't help but feel our future is a little more, secure. Do you know what I mean?
CHRISTINE 2	I know exactly what you mean. But I find it hard to imagine a time when your future wasn't secure. You have always been blessed with luck.

NORA 2	It's true I've been lucky in many ways.
CHRISTINE 2	In every way.
NORA 2	Not quite.
CHRISTINE 2	What do you mean?
NORA 2	It doesn't matter.
CHRISTINE 2	Nora?
NORA 2	I thought you wanted happy stories.
CHRISTINE 2	And after all these years, I would like to hear the truth too.
NORA 2	I'd choose happiness over the truth, wouldn't you?
CHRISTINE 2	No.
NORA 2	No? No. Yes. Of course. I was just being – silly.
	Are you looking for a man? At the moment? In the market for a boyfriend?
CHRISTINE 2	Not particularly.
NORA 2	Oh. Then you must work?
CHRISTINE 2	When I can find it. Bookkeeping and such. Though it's getting tougher to find, I fear I am not exactly what employers are looking for, a little – much, maybe. And I'd get one of those new credit cards except they still make it so hard for a woman to… never mind.
NORA 2	I've got an idea. Tom is bound to be looking for staff at some point – I could ask him if there might be something for you?
CHRISTINE 2	No. I wouldn't ask that of you.
NORA 2	Please. Let me help you? Let me help an old friend.

CHRISTINE 2   You mustn't go to any trouble.

NORA 2   It's no trouble.

CHRISTINE 2   Well, then... thank you. Thank you. If there
                was a little something for me, I would
                gladly take it.

NORA 2   Then I'll ask him. You must feel very proud
                to work. I've never... I've never.

CHRISTINE 2   I like it. It gives me – options. I don't
                believe money makes you happy, but it
                certainly does give you options. And it also
                gives me purpose. Because the truth is
                sometimes, Nora. Sometimes I feel so...
                I feel ever so, well, you know.

NORA 2   No. I don't.

CHRISTINE 2   Then you must be very happy. Very proud to
                keep a home.

NORA 2   You think I am foolish?

CHRISTINE 2   No, never. A woman can do as she wishes.
                Tell me then, what are you most proud of?
                Your children?

NORA 2   Yes. I suppose.

CHRISTINE 2   You're uncertain?

NORA 2   No. Well...

CHRISTINE 2   Do I sense a secret?

NORA 2   No, I...

CHRISTINE 2   Tell me! We must always talk the truth to
                each other.

NORA 2   Well. If we are talking of the truth.

CHRISTINE 2   Always.

NORA 2	You're right. The thing I feel most proud of is – a secret. A secret, that if I am going to share it, you must swear to keep it and not even share it with your shadow.
CHRISTINE 2	I swear.
NORA 2	And she explains that there was a time when her husband was very ill. He lay in bed for months, unable and fading – for reasons that fail her.
NORA 3	Because it was something to do with the pressure of the world changing. He had spent just a few months in France, far enough away from the front line so as to keep all his fingers. But it seems part of him had been damaged because he never did stop jumping at the sound of doors slamming.
NORA 2	The Swinging Sixties seem to have swung in a direction away from him. The traditions he clung on to were crumbling, so he found himself stumbling to find his place in this new landscape.
NORA 1	Because magazines and the TV and the internet and just about everyone he met reminded him of all the things he lacked. Because he didn't own his house or his car and even their furniture was on credit. Which meant there was nothing for him to hold on to when he fell into a state of sadness.
NORA 3	Simply put – he fell apart and so did their finances. And even their savings shrivelled up soon enough.
NORA 1	But they kept on spending and selling the lie that everything was fine.
NORA 2	Because she didn't want her children to worry.

NORA 3	And she didn't want her neighbours to know.
NORA 1	And as she tells her friend of her husband's difficulties and their debt, water wets her eyes, but she is determined not to cry.
CHRISTINE 2	That's awful, Nora. How did you keep it all together? How did you... keep all this?
NORA 2	I used to tell people – it was my inheritance seeing us through those dark times. My father had just died, you see, and I said his wallet was our protection. When actually he died without much to his name.
CHRISTINE 2	Oh, I'm so /
NORA 2	It was me. I raised that money. I – and I alone – covered our bills and expenses and... everything. For months and months, I didn't just keep a home, I ran it. I ran this whole household – like a man. And that, is what I am most proud of and I've never told anyone, until now.
CHRISTINE 2	I'm honoured that you told me. And that's incredible. I mean – that must have been a huge amount of money. How did you get it?
NORA 2	Well, I arranged to – wait. No. That. That I won't say. Some secrets – must stay secrets. I must be careful not to get too giddy.
CHRISTINE 2	Why? You haven't done something silly? Have you? To get the money.
NORA 2	Is it silly to save your whole family?
CHRISTINE 2	Then why lie and say it's your father's money? And am I right in saying, not even Tom knows about this? Nora. What have you done?
NORA 2	I did what I had to.

CHRISTINE 2   And what is that?

NORA *remains silent. She smiles and shrugs.*

Well, I am sorry to hear about your father, I know you were very fond of him. But I am glad to hear those terrible times have passed, it's impressive that Tom has this new job, considering he was so ill.

NORA 2   It is amazing what you can be capable of, when you try.

CHRISTINE 2   And I never knew you were capable of such secrets.

NORA 2   I felt capable. Christine. In secrecy and silence, I saved my whole family and maybe for the first time in my life, I felt capable.

CHRISTINE 2   Well, that's a wonderful thing. And it's brave. What you have done, for your husband, your children.

NORA 2   Do you really think that?

CHRISTINE 2   I think being brave can look like many things and most of them are unexpected.

NORA 2   Oh, I have missed you. I have missed having someone to talk to.

CHRISTINE 2   And I realise it's ridiculous to turn up out of the blue but I'm... well, I'm glad I did.

NORA 2   Yes. I'm glad too.

Silence.

CHRISTINE 2   I suddenly need a cigarette. Do you mind?

NORA 2   No, of course not.

CHRISTINE 2   I shall go out to the garden – would hate to ruin this lovely smell. Lavender? Is it?

NORA 2	Yes. Lavender. You saw the door through the kitchen?
	CHRISTINE *nods and turns to leave.*
	And Christine? Why today? Why visit today, after all this time.
CHRISTINE 2	I am visiting an old friend of my mother's and I'd heard you lived nearby and I… I was always so sad we had fallen out of touch. I missed you. I suppose, I missed you. I won't be a moment.
	CHRISTINE *leaves. A knock at the door.* NORA *answers the door – it's* NATHAN.
NORA 3	Mr McKinnon.
NATHAN 3	Good afternoon, Mrs Helmer.
NORA 3	What brings you to my door?
NATHAN 3	I am here to talk to your husband. I believe he is to be above me in the bank. So, I want to wish him well.
NORA 3	And that is the only reason for your visit?
NATHAN 3	You will raise suspicion if you look any more concerned about my arrival, Mrs Helmer.
NORA 3	And what would I have to be suspicious about?
NATHAN 3	Then are you not better to place a smile on your face?
NORA 3	I always have a smile on my face, Mr McKinnon.
NATHAN 3	Then won't you invite me in? There is a sharp chill in the air.
	NORA *reluctantly lets him in.*

	That river is set to freeze over. You should be mindful of your children playing near it.
NORA 3	How thoughtful of you to mention that to me.
NATHAN 3	I'm surprised that weather did not stop you ladies from voting.
NORA 3	It would have taken more than a little chill to stop us from voting for the first time.
NATHAN 3	It seems as though this year has turned out to be a year for the history books. They will be writing about it until the next century.
NORA 3	Women voting and the end of a war are things certainly worth celebrating. Remind me, where was it you served, Mr McKinnon?
NATHAN 3	Have we not had this conversation before?
NORA 3	It must have slipped my mind.
NATHAN 3	Unfortunately, I did not get the opportunity to serve my country, on account of my /
NORA 3	Failings?
NATHAN 3	Children. Widowers with children were exempt from service. Tell me, did you enjoy your first fluttering with the vote?
NORA 3	Yes. I did.
NATHAN 3	You'll do well to remember that politics are a mirage. They make you think that you can change things. When you cannot.
NORA 3	Clearly that isn't true.
NATHAN 3	But how many times have I voted and how many times have I got the country I wanted?
NORA 3	Mr Helmer is in the back room.
NATHAN 3	Is my talk not small enough for someone like /

NORA 3	Thomas is in the back room.
NATHAN 3	Thank you, Nora.
	NATHAN *leaves*. NORA *is left for a moment*.
	CHRISTINE *enters*.
CHRISTINE 3	Oh, Nora. Your kitchen is lovely. Very... yellow. That wallpaper is certainly... something.
NORA 3	Thank you, Christine. It's a little old-fashioned but Thomas likes it that way
CHRISTINE 3	There is a sudden chill in here.
NORA 3	I had the door open.
CHRISTINE 3	A visitor?
NORA 3	A Mr McKinnon.
CHRISTINE 3	Nathan?
NORA 3	You know him?
CHRISTINE 3	I used to... many years ago. It appears my past is surrounding me.
	DANIEL *walks in from the room next door*.
DANIEL 3	(*Calling back to* THOMAS.) I shall see myself out.
NORA 3	Daniel! You've appeared like magic.
DANIEL 3	A simple trick, I slipped in the back door. When I looked through the window and I saw you both talking I did not wish to get in the way.
NORA 3	Oh, but you are always welcome here. Christine, this is our friend Daniel. He lives just around this corner. He works at the chemist and helps keep us all fighting fit. And this is Christine, an old friend.

CHRISTINE 3	It is lovely to meet you.
DANIEL 3	And a pleasure to finally meet you. I've heard so much about you.
NORA 3	Can you believe it's been a nearly a century since I last saw her.
CHRISTINE 3	You mean nearly a decade, Nora.
NORA 3	Of course, how foolish of me.
DANIEL 3	Speaking of fools, your husband is entertaining the company of one.
CHRISTINE 3	Nathan McKinnon?
DANIEL 3	Walked straight in on us in the middle of our conversation. Not even a knock. He wished to congratulate Thomas on his new position in the bank. You'll do well not to let him visit again. Mr McKinnon rather has a reputation.
CHRISTINE 3	Do we not all have reputations?
DANIEL 3	His wife drank herself to death, drowned in cheap gin. He was left alone with his two children. Barely managing to /
NORA 3	Enough. We should be celebrating the end of this tremendous year. In fact, we've absolutely no choice – let us raise a glass of something.
DANIEL 3	I thought you were trying to drink a little less?
NORA 3	Christine brought it.
CHRISTINE 3	Did I?
NORA 3	Let us all have one – two at most. But three does sound like fun.

NORA reaches into her shopping and pulls out the bottle of alcohol, pours them all a drink.

Let us raise a toast to peacetime.

CHRISTINE 3   And progress.

DANIEL 3   And pals.

NORA 3   Pals? What a word, Daniel. But what a wonderful word.

ALL   To peacetime, progress and pals!

They savour it. THOMAS *enters holding his jacket.*

NORA 3   Shhhhhh....

NORA quietly and playfully hides the bottle.

THOMAS 3   Do I sense secrets?

NORA 3   No such thing.

DANIEL 3   Did you get rid of him?

THOMAS 3   I walked him out the back door. Are you having a tipple?

NORA quickly interjects.

NORA 3   Thomas, please let me introduce you to Christine – a friend from school.

THOMAS 3   I do not believe we've met.

THOMAS *and* CHRISTINE *shake hands.*

CHRISTINE 3   I have heard a lot about you.

THOMAS 3   I should hope nothing but kind words.

NORA 3   Of course! In fact, she has travelled all this way just to meet you.

CHRISTINE 3   Well…

NORA 3   Christine has always been good with numbers – ever since we were children. And she is looking for a job that she could grow into and better herself. I thought maybe you are the very person to help her. I have never known someone get so far on their own steam as you – brilliant you. Do you think there might be something for her?

THOMAS 3   You have experience of bookkeeping?

CHRISTINE 3   Plenty.

THOMAS 3   And you have no husband or /

CHRISTINE 3   No. I am alone, in those respects.

THOMAS 3   Well. You will need to interview of course but I am certain we can organise something.

NORA 3   I knew it.

CHRISTINE 3   Oh, how can I thank you?

THOMAS 3   There is no need to. But I do need to go the bank I have more files to collect and read. By the time I start in January I need to know the place like I was born in the boardroom.

NORA 3   You work so ceaselessly for us.

THOMAS 3   Like any husband or father, would or should.

DANIEL 3   I'll walk with you.

THOMAS 3   Are you on your way to work, Daniel?

DANIEL 3   No. I… I am due a day off.

THOMAS 3   Quite right. You work so hard and are looking tired for it.

DANIEL 3   It's true, I have been tired recently. But nothing your company does not fix.

	THOMAS *and* CHRISTINE *puts on their jackets*.
CHRISTINE 3	I should also be on my way.
NORA 3	I could make up a bed for you here?
CHRISTINE 3	You have done more than enough for me. I'm staying with a friend of my mother's. It's very nearby.
DANIEL 3	Until tomorrow.
NORA 3	Until tomorrow. And Christine, shall I see you tomorrow? Will you come by?
CHRISTINE 3	That would be lovely.
THOMAS 3	Nora, will you fetch the children? You know how I hate them playing down by that river. It is an accident waiting to happen.
NORA 3	Yes. Of course. Goodbye. Stay warm.
THOMAS 3	So long, skylark.
	THOMAS *kisses her on the forehead*. THOMAS, CHRISTINE *and* DANIEL *leave, talking*.
NORA 3	A woman's finger falls to her wrist and she feels a small cut from only a few days ago. A small cut from when she stood in the ballot box and for the first time had her future at her fingertips. She gripped that pencil so tight her thumb went numb. The lead snapped as she placed it on the paper. And she marked it with her heart and her head and her hope. She marked it with hope. Then she rolled down her glove and took the piece of paper and gently glided it along her skin. A thin sting of red, rose to the surface. A paper cut. She ensured it was deep enough to scar as she thought of that

woman lying dead in front of a horse and
a king, so she could stand here and for the
very first time have her future at her
fingertips. She stared at the red ribbon of
blood that lined the bottom of her ballot
paper and wondered about all the things we
was willing to bleed for – 'Oh, silly me' is
what she said when she got home, and
pretended it was an accident. 'Oh, silly me.'

A knock at the door. NORA *opens it – it's*
NATHAN.

NORA 1	Nathan? Twice in one day. Lucky me.
NATHAN 1	I'm just /
NORA 1	He isn't home. Tommy's gone into town.
NATHAN 1	It isn't him I'm after. It's you.

NORA *hesitates. She lets him in.*

	That woman? That woman who just left here… that was Christine. Wasn't it?
NORA 1	So, what if it was?
NATHAN 1	Heard she is going through hard times. Heard she is struggling to find work, lost her man too.
NORA 1	People go through hard times, Nathan. It's what they do – they go through hard times.
NATHAN 1	You know what I also heard?
NORA 1	That you're a good listener?
NATHAN 1	You're quick.
NORA 1	And you're not quick enough because I need to get my kids indoors.
NATHAN 1	Your husband doesn't think much of me. That's what I heard. He proved as much this

afternoon. Hardly said two things and he was shoving me out the door. Rumour has it when he starts, he is going to fire some folk – something about letting go of old history.

NORA 1   What's this got to do with me?

NATHAN 1   Well. When I see Christine is busy walking down the street with your husband, I can't help but feel she is looking for a new man or a new job. And you're still wearing your wedding ring.

NORA 1   Don't you think you're jumping to conclusions?

NATHAN 1   No. I know how the world works. You only get pulled up and out of the shit if you know the hand doing the pulling. And I just want to make sure my job is safe and I'm not losing it, so Christine can get hers.

NORA 1   I'm not... how can you expect me to /

NATHAN 1   Just say you'll help.

NORA 1   Help how?

NATHAN 1   Just say you'll help me.

NORA (*all*)   There is nothing I can do.

NATHAN 1   Are you sure about that?

NORA 1   Why?

NATHAN 1   Here. Take this.

          NATHAN *holds out a document*. NORA *takes it.*

NORA 3   And he hands her a document. Ready for this moment when...

NORA 2   This moment when /

NORA 1   This moment when /

NATHAN 1	I know what you did. And here is the proof.
	NORA *opens the envelope and looks at the pieces of paper. She stands – shocked.*
NORA 3	And in her hand was a copy of a loan agreement.
NORA 2	A successful credit-card application.
NORA 1	A payday-loan contract.
NORA (*all*)	What is this?
NATHAN 1	Those papers were signed by your dad. We got his application in the post. He clearly needed a lot of cash and quickly. Which is surprising because I checked the dates and dying men don't tend to need so much money.
NORA 1	They must have got the dates wrong.
NORA 2	And he never was very good with his finances.
NORA 3	So, why are you showing this to me?
NATHAN 1	The papers were submitted just days before he died and wasn't he terribly sick? And if he was anything like my father, I bet he wasn't even conscious in those final days. It wouldn't take much to find out and it wouldn't take much to counterfeit a dying man's signature.
NORA (*all*)	What?
NATHAN 1	Not to mention there is a trail of unsuccessful applications in your name. You couldn't get the money – so you pretended to be him. It's easy enough to prove you committed fraud, Nora. I know you're a thief.

NORA 3	Forged.
NORA 2	Faked.
NORA 1	Fucked.
	NORA *rips up the letter.*
NATHAN 1	You think that's the only copy?
NORA 1	You're blackmailing me?
NATHAN 1	It's clever really, what you did.
NORA 1	How did you know?
NATHAN 1	I've got access to all the accounts. Trust me, information is easy to find when you go looking. And, don't look at me like that, not like that, because I'm not the one looking at time in prison.
NORA (*all*)	Prison?
NATHAN 1	Minimum two years, but it could be more. Or maybe, they'd just put you under house arrest, but I wonder if they'd take away your kids? Regardless, I imagine a criminal record could really fuck things up for you. Not to mention your husband's new job.
NORA (*all*)	Oh my god.
NATHAN 1	And I'll show everyone what you did. I'll show everyone who you really are. Unless I can keep my job.
NORA 1	But it's just a job and this is my whole life.
NATHAN 1	You're right it's a stupid shit job that makes poor people poorer. But do you know how long it took me to get that fucking job? A lifetime. A whole fucking lifetime. Don't let them take that away from me.
NORA 1	But I don't know how to help you.

NATHAN 1	Then find a way.
NORA 1	But... please... I never wanted to... I was just trying to... Tommy was sick and we had bills to pay and quickly and... I was trying to... I was desperate.
NATHAN 1	Oh. I know. I know what desperate is. Everyone around here knows what desperate is and I don't want to hurt you, Nora. All I want to be is a good father, with a good job but the world makes that so fucking hard.
NORA 1	The world makes lots of things fucking hard. So, please. Please don't do this... I'll do anything. Please. I'll do anything you want. Anything... please. If you want someone,.... I'd sleep with you – you can do anything you want to me – fuck me however you want, I don't care... I don't care... please, just /
NATHAN 1	Once you know my job is safe, Nora. You can come and tell me. You come and knock on my door and tell me the good news. And I'll destroy any proof of... anything. That way we're both safe. And you'll know what door to knock, it's the only yellow door on the street. You know, I fucking hate it but it was my wife's favourite colour. She painted that door and my kids won't let me /
NORA 1	But what about my kids?
NATHAN 1	And what about mine. Because I will do anything to keep them safe. They are the only reason, the only reason, I haven't drowned myself in that river. I imagine you'd say the same.
	Silence.

NORA 1	If I got money – could I pay you off? If not the job... then money?
NATHAN 1	It would need to be a hell of a lot of money. Double, triple, what you borrowed.
NORA 1	That's impossible.
NATHAN 1	Then make sure I keep my job.
NORA 1	Please.
NATHAN 1	Stop begging. Your husband might treat you like one, but you're not a dog.
NORA 1	But... please.
NATHAN 1	Money is fucking awful isn't it? The things it does to us. The things it's already done.
	NATHAN *hesitates*.
	I'm going to leave now, but I'm wanting to hear from you soon. Merry Christmas. Nora.
	NATHAN *leaves*. NORA *is left*.
NORA 2	A criminal.
NORA 3	Everything?
NORA 1	I just...
NORA 2	The children...
NORA 1	I just...
NORA 3	We'd lose everything.
NORA 2	I can't.
NORA 1	I just...
NORA (*all*)	What have I done?
	Silence. THOMAS *enters*.
THOMAS 3	The children are asking for you. You really should not let them play outdoors for so long. Did you have company?

NORA *shakes her head.*

Are you sure... because I walked past
Mr McKinnon. Fresh snow, Nora. His
footprints led back to here.

NORA 3   He stepped in for a few minutes.

THOMAS 3   Did he mention he is worried about the
                security of his employment? And asked you
                to put in a good word for him? Your face,
                my songbird. It tells me truths.

NORA 3   Does it?

She turns away from him.

THOMAS 3   I say that in jest, Nora. I heard at the bank
                he has been voicing concerns about his
                position. But you were not going to tell me
                he visited, were you? You should be careful,
                secrets and lies are like damp. Once they are
                in the woodwork, the whole house is
                condemned. And don't allow yourself to
                believe that there is a scrap of human in
                him. He would happily tread on anyone if
                he thought it helped him.

NORA 3   Do you think he would harm someone?
                Really, truly?

THOMAS 3   Oh, my little songbird, life in this sitting
                room is very different to life on a street.
                In here is a haven and I am thankful for it.
                Thankful for you.

NORA 3   Thomas?

THOMAS 3   What?

NORA 3   What did he do? Why does everyone seem
                to dislike him so?

THOMAS 3   He borrowed money from anyone who
                would listen and never paid it back.

NORA 3   There are worse crimes.

THOMAS 3   He bankrupted his whole family. Took every
              penny of his mother's and sold half of her
              belongings without her permission. And if
              you are to believe rumours – which I do not
              – he was once wrapped up with some rather
              unfavourable gambling types. Not to
              mention his wife drank her life away. Poor
              life choices.

NORA 3   He sounds desperate.

THOMAS 3   Morally bankrupt if you ask me.

NORA 3   But it seems he can keep a job and raise his
              two children. Maybe he has changed? Do
              people not deserve second chances?

THOMAS 3   Not men like him.

NORA 3   But, his poor family.

THOMAS 3   Exactly. Just last week one of children was
              picked up by the police for stealing. Those
              children have been affected by their father's
              terrible choices. I mean poor parenting
              leaves very particular scars – do you not
              you think? Children are like sponges. They
              soak up more than we can imagine.

NORA 3   You really think that?

THOMAS 3   I know it. Look what our fathers did to us.

NORA 3   I loved my father.

THOMAS 3   But do we not love people despite their
              flaws?

NORA 3   Or because of them?

THOMAS 3   You always reach for the positive no matter
              how implausible. Which is why I am so
              pleased our children have you. They are

only around your goodness and sweetness.
Not contaminated by someone else's terrible
choices. And regardless, I'm going to ask
for Mr Nathan McKinnon to be dismissed in
the new year.

NORA (*all*)   No.

THOMAS 3   Yes.

NORA 3   No. You can't. You can't do that.

THOMAS 3   Why should it concern you?

NORA 2   Please, Thomas.

NORA 1   You've got to give him a second chance.

THOMAS 3   He isn't worth your worry.

NORA (*all*)   No.

THOMAS 3   Nora.

NORA 3   No.

THOMAS 3   Nora.

NORA 1   Please don't.

NORA 2   Please.

NORA 3   You can't.

THOMAS 3   Nora – keep calm. You'll make yourself
panicked and recently, you have been very
good at keeping yourself calm. And it
speaks to your kindness that you could care
so much about the fate of stranger. But you
must forget him.

And don't frown, it will give you wrinkles.

Silence.

NORA 3   Thomas?

THOMAS 3   Yes?

NORA 3	There has been… I seemed to have… I have…
THOMAS 3	You must be tired from your day. You can barely string two words together.
NORA 3	I need your help.
THOMAS 3	I already said I would bring down the decorations when I had time.
NORA 3	No. It's…
THOMAS 3	What? I have enough to stew on without your silly little worries.

Silence. NORA *hesitates.*

NORA 3	A dress. For the party we are attending. It's only two days away and I do not know what to wear.
THOMAS 3	No need to go watery-eyed at the thought of picking a dress. I will help you. But first – a drink. And call in the children, won't you. They should come in, be around you and your warmth.

THOMAS *leaves. Silence.*

NORA 1	A woman stands alone in her sitting room. Surprised by how destructive she has been.
NORA 2	How in attempting to save everything she has snapped it.
NORA 3	In silence and secrecy she has destroyed, everything.
NORA 1	And she is astounded by her own power.
NORA 2	She never knew she had it in her.
NORA 3	My skeleton.
NORA 2	My ribcage.

NORA 1	My heart.
NORA 3	As if /
NORA 1	As if /
NORA 3	As if it was enough just to feel it.
NORA 2	As if it was enough just to feel it to stop it.
NORA 1	Can feel myself pollute.
NORA 3	Can feel myself turn to poison at the thought.
NORA 1	From milk into madness and back again.
NORA 2	Curdling and turning and craving. As if my hands were enough to hold back any hurt.
NORA 3	As if my hands were /
NORA 2	Would dig through all of hellfire.
NORA 1	Would walk barefooted through sleet and snow.
NORA 2	Would do /
NORA 3	Would do just about /
NORA 1	My heart beats for /
NORA (*all*)	My heart beats for you.
NORA 1	And as she thinks of her children.
NORA 3	She thinks of the river.
NORA 2	She thinks of being washed clean.
NORA 1	Stay out there, kids. Play as long as you'd like.
NORA 2	Children. It's good to get fresh air.
NORA 3	My sweethearts. Keep playing.
NORA (*all*)	Be careful of that river and just stay out there. Stay away from me.

DAY TWO

NORA 2

A woman walks into her living room after a sleepless dreamless night to find that her children had got up early to make a Christmas card just for her. It's all glue and glitter and their attempts at artistry pull at parts of her that feel like the most fragile. It's been years since she stood outside the doctor's office with her hand on her stomach. For the third time something was growing inside of her. The third time – no monthly bleeding, the morning sickness, a tiredness trapped in every tendon. There was a sense of purpose she enjoyed about being pregnant. But sometimes she just felt like a body that needed prodded and measured and ripped open when the time was right. And she knew that more mouths need more money. More money meant less of her husband and less of her husband meant… well, an afternoon can feel like a precariously long time when you are the only adult. And when that third child arrived, through a slit in her stomach. It took twenty-six stitches to sew her up. Stitches that she picked at, and although it hurt, she still played with the strands that stuck out of her. All dried blood and sore skin. Now, a scar stretched and stubborn sits there on her stomach. Her husband won't touch it, but it still fascinates her. And she thinks about how a human can heal from being torn in two. And as tears fill her eyes and her children question why, she replies – 'Mummy is just being silly, just being silly.'

CHRISTINE 2	Afternoon, Nora!
NORA 2	Oh, Christine.
CHRISTINE 2	It's just me. No need to be alarmed.
NORA 2	I've been a million miles away all day.
CHRISTINE 2	Is everything fine?
NORA 2	I am… overwhelmingly fine.
CHRISTINE 2	There is such a thing?
NORA 2	Of course.
	Did you see the children playing? They insisted on going outside again to finish whatever game they were playing yesterday. I watch them from the window, how I wish I could play pretend like they do.
CHRISTINE 2	Oh, Nora. Adults still have their games.
NORA 2	I suppose they might, I actually wanted to ask you something. We are going to a party tomorrow and I want to wear a very particular dress, but the trouble is last time I wore it I managed to catch it on something and it tore. And I have been trying all morning to /
CHRISTINE 2	It won't take me long with a needle and thread to sort that out.
NORA 2	How did you know? Am I that useless?
CHRISTINE 2	No. Of course not, I was just… you are entirely lovely. And if you are useless then I must be too.
	They look at each other a little too long.
	While walking here I saw your friend – Daniel? He looked… well… I can't say he looked very well at all.

NORA 2	No, he isn't a well man, he has been poorly since he was young. His father was an awful man – for all the reasons fathers can be awful. It's really rather remarkable he survived his childhood.
CHRISTINE 2	It is remarkable any of us survive our childhoods.
NORA 2	Do you really think that?
CHRISTINE 2	Daniel said he had heard of me?
NORA 2	I must mention you, a lot. You were very important to me all those years ago. You still are important to me.
CHRISTINE 2	How can I be important when you haven't seen me in nearly a decade?
NORA 2	I suppose… I never forgot your face.
CHRISTINE 2	I have a forgettable face.
NORA 2	No. You don't.
CHRISTINE 2	I did wonder if he was your mysterious benefactor.
NORA 2	Daniel?
CHRISTINE 2	I noticed he wasn't wearing a wedding ring and he didn't speak of children. Unless of course… he prefers the company of other men.
NORA 2	Christine.
CHRISTINE 2	What?
NORA 2	You've jumped to a very particular conclusion.
CHRISTINE 2	It's been legal a whole year, Nora. And around a lot longer than that. Is it really so bad for two men to share a life? If anything

wouldn't it do us a favour if men lived with each other rather than us.

NORA 2   Well... I find it hard to imagine, is all. Who would do the dishes?

CHRISTINE 2   You are behind the times we live in, Nora. Or maybe, Thomas has kept you there. Tell me – is he the reason you don't work?

NORA 2   He would rather I raised the children.

CHRISTINE 2   And what would you rather?

The world is changing before our very eyes, Nora. Especially for us. We don't have to live the life of our mothers. Just look around, abortions – above-board – for the first time, this very year. And the contraceptive pill too, to stop children happening in the first place. Which is as close to a miracle as I will see this lifetime.

NORA 2   It is amazing to think you can undo a child. Such options, such options I never had.

CHRISTINE 2   What do you mean... do you think you might have /

NORA 2   No. Of course not. It's just... I was so terribly sad after the children were born. Sadness three times. I only just feel like I am returning to myself – after all these years and now... and now...

CHRISTINE 2   Has something happened since yesterday? You seem a little... undone.

Long silence.

NORA 2   I've laid everything out in the kitchen, everything you'll need to fix the dress.

CHRISTINE 2   Are you... are you alright /

NORA 2	Please make some tea or some coffee or a glass of whatever. I do appreciate your help.
CHRISTINE 2	Nora…
	Silence. THOMAS *enters, carrying folders and files. He places them down.*
NORA 2	My darling! You took your time!
THOMAS 2	It is rather icy out there.
CHRISTINE 2	More files to study, Tom?
THOMAS 2	It seems to be never-ending and I managed to forget my briefcase at home. My head is so full of facts and figures.
CHRISTINE 2	Then I'll leave you be and get to that sewing.
NORA 2	Thank you, Christine.
	CHRISTINE *exits.*
	I've invited her over to help fix my dress.
THOMAS 2	So, I chose well?
NORA 2	Yes. I'm glad I gave in to you.
THOMAS 2	Gave in to me?
NORA 2	I didn't mean /
THOMAS 2	I know what you meant.
NORA 2	You're working?
THOMAS 2	Of course. I still have so much to catch up on and January is less than two weeks away. And then our life will change, won't it?
NORA 2	I hope it doesn't change too much.
THOMAS 2	Well, of course. A new year, a new job, a beautiful wife and three fine children. What more could a man want.

NORA 2	It's… amazing. Isn't it? You've got everything you've ever wanted.
NORA (*all*)	And I am so proud of you.
THOMAS 2	What do you want?
NORA (*all*)	You are so suspicious.
THOMAS 2	Something tells me I have the right to be suspicious. What is it my songbird wants?
NORA 2	Would you be willing to grant me a wish? One last wish before the year is out.
THOMAS 2	What is it?
NORA 2	I'd be willing to do just about anything for it.
NORA 3	Your little skylark would sing for you – any song you wanted.
NORA 1	It's just a favour. I am not asking for a miracle.
THOMAS 2	Then what? What is it that has you fluttering?
NORA 2	Please… please will you let Mr McKinnon keep his job?
THOMAS 2	I am giving his job to Christine – isn't that what you wanted?
NORA 2	But isn't there room for both of them? Can't you get rid of someone else.
THOMAS 2	You know I do not understand you, Nora. Have you promised him something which I cannot deliver?
NORA 2	Who knows what he will say about you, he could spread lies and untruths. If he is as bad as you believe he is – why would you anger him? I don't think he would stop short of slandering your whole name.

NORA 3	We don't know what people are capable of – they could dig up anything, make up anything. Please, Thomas. Think of me, think of the children…
THOMAS 3	I am not scared of him.
NORA 3	Is it so bad to listen to your wife's opinion?
THOMAS 3	I can listen, but it does not mean I have to take it.
NORA (*all*)	Then please listen.
THOMAS 3	This is getting tiring.
NORA 3	You cannot dismiss a man who is good at his job. That is immoral.
THOMAS 3	Then what if I am making structural changes? Structural changes to his department. He cannot have his job if it no longer exists. And of course, he is free to apply for another position, but I imagine Christine, might have a little better luck, in fact why don't I just…
NORA 3	Thomas? What are you doing?
THOMAS 3	I shall get them to inform him of his notice period. I do not imagine there will be much resistance and it's one less task for January and you might finally stop mentioning him.
NORA 3	But it's Christmas and you haven't officially started your /
THOMAS 3	And this is business and trust me, people will be glad he is gone.
NORA 3	Please. Do not do this. Do not do this. You do not realise what this could do please.

NORA *grabs on to* THOMAS.

You have no idea what this could do.

THOMAS *shrugs off* NORA.

THOMAS 3	Oh please.
NORA 3	Do not, Thomas.

NORA *grabs on to* THOMAS *again.*

THOMAS 3	Stop it.
NORA 3	You don't know what this will do.
THOMAS 3	I said stop it.
NORA 3	You don't know /
THOMAS 3	And I said /
NORA (*all*)	Stop.

NORA *slaps* THOMAS. *Both are in shock. He backs away. She moves towards him.*

THOMAS 3	Nora.
NORA 3	Thomas, I am so sorry. I am so sorry. Forgive me. I was overwhelmed... something overwhelmed me, I... didn't mean to hurt you. I'm...
THOMAS 3	I do not... imagine the children walked in?
NORA 3	I am so sorry. I am so sorry for what I have done.

NORA *drops to her knees. Silence.*

THOMAS 3	What has gotten into you? What is with all this hysteria? You are acting like a madwoman over something which does not concern you.
NORA 3	I just... what if I were to tell you something. Something which... would change everything. Something which would... disappoint you. Greatly disappoint you.
THOMAS 3	Oh, please. Nora. I already know.

NORA (*all*)	What do you mean?
THOMAS 3	I already know, my little skylark. You cannot keep secrets from me.
	THOMAS *picks up* NORA.
	There is no need to get dirt on your knees.
NORA 3	You know?
THOMAS 3	Of course, I know.
	I know the children broke my mother's porcelain doll. I saw the chips on the floor last week and then I saw it was missing...
NORA 3	Oh.
THOMAS 3	Accidents happen. Even I can appreciate that. Is this what this is all this about? Is it? The air of guilt. The mania. All this madness over a broken doll. I know that you are very sensitive to these things. But this... this is out of all proportion. For you are not capable of true terribleness, Nora. I know that. Even the thought that you might be capable of a second of badness... it makes my whole heart hurt, like I am on the brink of a heart attack.
NORA 3	Do not say that.
THOMAS 3	You are goodness through and through, a delicate goodness. Like that little porcelain doll.
NORA 1	Tommy... I'm...
NORA (*all*)	I'm sorry.
NORA 2	I never meant to cause any... trouble.
THOMAS 2	How could I stay angry at that face? Now, what was I going to do... yes, Mr Nathan McKinnon. I do hope he goes without too

much fuss. I'll come back and put away those files and folders once I'm finished my phone call and, in the meantime, you should settle yourself. Maybe you should take one of your pills. Stop you from flying away.

THOMAS *exits*. NORA *is left*.

NORA 1	Must settle myself.
NORA 3	Must still my soul.
NORA 2	Silence these thoughts.
NORA 1	Silence these feelings.
NORA 3	Drown it out.
NORA 2	Flood it out.
NORA 1	Stop thinking these thoughts.
NORA (*all*)	Must drown it out.

A knock on the door. NORA *takes several large breaths and opens it. It's* DANIEL.

NORA 1	Danny.
DANIEL 1	Mind if I step in?
NORA 1	I'm actually... I'm in the middle of something.
DANIEL 1	Oh, right. It's just I... I saw the kids outside and figured you'd like some company.
NORA 1	I thought they might burn off some excess energy playing out here.
DANIEL 1	Oh, yeah. Sure...
NORA 1	Shouldn't you be at work?
DANIEL 1	Got someone to cover my shift at the chemist because it's just I...
NORA 1	You alright, Danny?

DANIEL 1   No. Not really.

Silence. NORA *hesitates.*

NORA 1   Come in. I wasn't... just come in. What's...
             what's wrong?

DANIEL 1   Everything.

NORA 1   That's not like you.

DANIEL 1   Yeah. Yeah. It's not like me but... I had
             a doctor's appointment this morning.

NORA 1   What?

DANIEL 1   Went to the doctor with a pain in my ribs
             I couldn't shift. Yeah? Just a pain I couldn't...
             so eventually I went to the doctor's.

NORA 1   Why didn't you say anything?

DANIEL 1   Because that's not like me.

NORA 1   You should have said something.

DANIEL 1   But it's not like me. And actually, I didn't
             want to tell you, but it seems I could barely
             step six inches into your home without it
             spilling out.

             They found something in my lungs.

             I thought – it being me, it would be nothing.
             I've had plenty to deal with already and this
             is just another thing I would deal with, but
             I got results back this morning... it's
             aggressive. The growth, the treatment, it's
             all very... aggressive is the word they kept
             using. Didn't your dad have /

NORA 1   Yeah. Lung cancer.

DANIEL 1   Nice guy? Your old man?

NORA 1   I mean he wasn't... perfect. Let me get
             Tommy /

DANIEL 1	No. I'd rather he didn't know.
NORA 1	But you've told me?
DANIEL 1	I'd like to keep it private.
NORA 1	Then why tell me?
DANIEL 1	Because I had to tell someone. Because it's a lot... you know... it's a lot. It's a lot to imagine being forgotten.
NORA 1	You won't be forgotten.
DANIEL 1	There isn't much to remember me by... I thought about a will. Drafting a will but then I realised I wouldn't have anybody to leave anything too. Not that there is much to leave. My mother's jewellery, maybe, there is some money in that. Maybe, I should sell it... leave all my money to charity. Do one last good thing. Or have one big last party. A real big piss-up.
NORA 1	You think it could be worth something?
DANIEL 1	I imagine it is worth something. Aquamarine. Isn't that what they call it? Little stones in her ring, like water.
	Silence.
NORA 1	What if...
DANIEL 1	What?
NORA 1	No, it's just...
DANIEL 1	Hey, now. I've had a good shot at living, now it's a chance to try the alternative.
NORA 1	Danny.
DANIEL 1	And if you think I'm not going to that party tomorrow – you're wrong. I'm going to drink and dance and sing and shout until... until I can't.

NORA 1	Then I'll dance with you… for you. Would you like that?
DANIEL 1	Any guy likes to be danced for.
NORA 1	Then I'd like to dance for you.
DANIEL 1	And what should I do for you?
	Silence. NORA *pulls up her dress to reveal her underwear.*
NORA 1	Look at these stockings. I'm going to be wearing these… I'm just trying them on while Christine fixes my dress.
	Tomorrow, only the feet will be seen… but I thought I'd try them on.
	Do you want to feel them?
DANIEL 1	Nora, I…
NORA 1	I'm asking if you want to feel them.
DANIEL 1	Have you been drinking?
NORA 1	No. It's just cheap perfume. Go on.
DANIEL 1	No. Nora it's…
NORA 2	You can do it.
NORA 3	I know you want to.
DANIEL 1	But what if…
NORA 3	I do not mind.
DANIEL 1	Your eyes are glassy.
NORA 2	It's just the light.
NORA 1	I'm saying it's alright.
NORA 3	I'm giving you my permission.
DANIEL 1	Then I would like to touch you… very much.
NORA (*all*)	After all, it's just… skin.

NORA 1	Just skin.

He rubs his hand down her leg. His eyes close. She is steely with a sense that she is fighting back tears. She talks as he rubs.

Suppose I were to ask you... for something...

DANIEL 1	Anything. Ask me, anything.
NORA 1	Are you sure?
DANIEL 1	Tell me what you want.

His hand reaches her feet.

NORA 1	Again.
DANIEL 1	No. Nora it's...
NORA 2	You can do it.
NORA 3	I know you want to.
DANIEL 1	But what if...
NORA 3	I do not mind.
DANIEL 1	Your eyes are glassy.
NORA 2	It's just the light.
NORA 1	I'm saying it's alright.
NORA 3	I'm giving you my permission.
DANIEL 1	Then I would like to touch you... very much.
NORA (*all*)	After all, it's just... skin.
NORA 1	Just skin.

He rubs his hand down her leg. His eyes close. She is steely with a sense that she is fighting back tears. His hand reaches her feet.

DANIEL 2	Thank you.

NORA 2	I need something, Dan.
DANIEL 2	Tell me. Tell me what you need and if I can, I will give it to you.
NORA 2	But, if it's too much you must /
DANIEL 2	You've no idea, do you?
NORA 2	What?
DANIEL 2	I said to myself I would let you know before I... ever since I met you, I've had these feelings for you... not simple feelings either... not just wanting to touch you... not just that but wanting to... no, it's not that simple, because... I love you, Nora. I think I've always loved you.
NORA 2	Love?
DANIEL 2	Don't you know what it means to want something? Secretly?
NORA 2	I can imagine.
DANIEL 2	Have I spoilt everything?
NORA 2	No. No. I'm just... surprised.
DANIEL 2	I didn't mean to shock you.
NORA 2	No, it's...
DANIEL 2	What is it you wanted? Because I'd like to... if I can... help.
	Silence.
NORA 2	No. Dan. It wasn't anything important. You've got enough to deal with. It was silly of me to... I think Tom is smoking outside.
DANIEL 2	Then I'll go join him. Though I suppose I should think about stopping... if there is a point to that.
NORA 2	Don't you have hope?

DANIEL 2	No. Hope, can be so cruel. Don't you think?
	He goes to leave.
NORA 2	Dan? I'm sorry.
DANIEL 2	For what?
	You are worth love, Nora. I suddenly got a sense you don't think that. You are worth love.
	DANIEL *leaves.*
NORA 1	And as her breath is pulled out of her.
NORA 2	In the distance she can hear the river.
NORA 3	Calling to her. Calming her.
NORA 1	And she wonders – if this is everything.
NORA 2	Just everything.
NORA 3	And there is nothing more.
	A knock on the door. NORA *opens it – it's* NATHAN.
	Nathan.
	He just stands there, unable to talk.
	Nathan.
NATHAN 3	Structural changes? Structural changes. You cannot just take a man's job. Tell him he has just four weeks left at work. Four weeks' worth of pay and… I got the message not even an hour ago. Did you even try to stop him?
NORA 3	Please know, I tried my /
NATHAN 3	And you do not have money either – do you?
NORA 1	And she has no reply.
NORA 2	She has nothing to offer him.

NORA 3	To this man who is so willing to ruin everything.
NATHAN 3	All I want is a life worth living. All I want is my children to be safe and secure in their future.
NORA 1	But she couldn't, and she can't.
NORA 2	She couldn't, and she can't control him.
NORA 3	She couldn't, and she can't control any of them.
NATHAN 3	But your husband has taken that from me, so I am taking everything from you. Here is the proof. With a letter, detailing everything you have done. I will send one to the police and here is a copy for your husband.

NATHAN *pulls out a letter.*

NORA 3	I will not give it to him.
NORA 2	I'll rip the telephone out the wall.
NORA 1	I'll drown his phone.
NATHAN 3	You cannot stop me. Because all I would do is find another way.
NORA 3	He will see your name on the letter and hunt you down.
NATHAN 3	The letter is anonymous, there is no evidence it is me.
NORA 3	And if I destroy it?
NATHAN 3	Then he will find out from the police turning up at your door. So, I suppose this letter is an opportunity to have the conversation on your own terms. Before you cannot.
NORA 3	You talk like it is an act of charity. You are deluded.

NATHAN 3	Probably.
	And tomorrow. Tomorrow. I shall send the same letter to the police with the evidence of what you have done. Because at least that gives you a chance to kiss your children goodbye. I am giving you that.
NORA 1	If I go to prison, I'll die. Nathan.
NORA 2	It will kill me.
NORA 3	It will tear me in two.
NATHAN 3	My old man used to say debt is a form of death, suppose he is right.
	Good luck, Nora. Good luck to us all.
	NATHAN *places the letter down and leaves,* NORA *watches it.*
NORA 1	And out of nowhere, a woman has a desperate need to be held by her dad. A dad who died years ago. But the memory and the need of his arms are so clear in her mind it almost knocks her to her knees. But it doesn't, she just stands tracing a sliver of a scar from last Christmas. A Christmas she could barely afford. A Christmas that pushed her to the red line of no return. A Christmas full of tantrums and tired kids and broken toys and too much to drink and not enough money though she did enjoy the fluttering and fancying over new things. She got a buzz from buying and busying herself. And when she couldn't afford any more, she'd spend her last collection of coins on a Lottery ticket and crossed her fingers for the chance to change everything. And that night when her numbers didn't come up, and all she could think about was the spending and the crying and the drinking, she stood

washing her wine glass. One of the few thin
and delicate things in her home. And just as
she went to rinse it, she held it a little too
tight and it broke in her hand and a tiny
piece of glass pierced her palm. The
washing-up water slowly turned red. All
slow motion and sadness and she watched
the foam flicker with bright-red bubbles. She
was left with a cut in the shape of a 'C'. 'C'
for Christmas she thinks. 'C' for children.
'C' for careful. 'C' for cunt. 'C' for can't.
'C' for can't do this. 'C' for can't do this any
more. 'C' for can't breathe. 'C' for can't
breathe. 'C' for I can't breathe any more.
'C' for I can't breathe any more. 'C' for…

CHRISTINE *enters*.

Christine?

CHRISTINE 1	Done. Your dress is as good as new. What's wrong? You look like you've seen a ghost.
NORA 1	Nathan.
CHRISTINE 1	What about him?
NORA 1	That money? He knows how I got it and is blackmailing me, because I…
NORA 3	I have done something terrible, Christine. And he knows what.
NORA 2	Nathan is threatening to tell the police what I have done.
NORA 1	Fraud. Christine. I am a…
CHRISTINE 1	What?
NORA (*all*)	A thief.
NORA 2	I want you to be my witness.
CHRISTINE 2	To what?

NORA 2	If I should lose my mind and they try to blame Thomas. Tell them it was my fault.
NORA 3	I am the one who poisoned this family.
NORA 1	I brought this fucking shit into this house.
CHRISTINE 2	What are you saying?
NORA 2	I did this all by myself.
NORA 1	I have wrecked this family.
NORA 3	Destroyed everything.
CHRISTINE 1	Nora. Please let me help.
CHRISTINE 2	Nora, calm yourself.
CHRISTINE 3	Nora, there is one thing I can do.
CHRISTINE (*all*)	I'll go and talk to Nathan.
NORA (*all*)	No, Christine, don't!
CHRISTINE (*all*)	Let me try and help.
NORA (*all*)	He'll only hurt you too.
CHRISTINE (*all*)	Trust me. Nora. He won't hurt me.
NORA 2	What do you mean?
NORA 1	Christine? Why wouldn't he hurt you?
NORA 3	He only lives around the corner – I think. I don't know.
THOMAS (*all*)	(*Offstage.*) Nora!
NORA 1	Don't come in!
NORA 2	I'm trying on my dress!
NORA 3	I am not ready.
THOMAS (*all*)	(*Offstage.*) In the living room?
NORA 1	Don't come in!
NORA 3	Please, Thomas. Give me a minute.

NORA 2	Wait! The house with the yellow door. He told me that... there is only one house with a yellow door... please be quick.
THOMAS (*all*)	(*Offstage.*) Nora?
CHRISTINE 3	I promise, Nora. I'll do my very best. I'll run as fast as I can.

NORA *grabs on to* CHRISTINE.

NORA 2	Thank you. Thank you. Thank you.
CHRISTINE 2	Of course, my – sweetheart.
NORA 2	Christine, I just...

NORA *kisses* CHRISTINE, *on the lips, hard.* NORA *is shocked at her own actions and lets go.*

I'm sorry. I'm so... sorry.

CHRISTINE 2	No.
THOMAS 2	(*Offstage.*) Nora?

The two women are held in a moment.

(*Offstage.*) I'm waiting...

CHRISTINE 2	My dearest Nora.
NORA 2	Christine... I...
CHRISTINE 2	I'll be as quick as I can.

CHRISTINE *exits.* THOMAS *enters.*

THOMAS 2	I thought you were changing?
NORA 2	I was... changing out of it. You can't see me in my dress before tomorrow. Isn't that bad luck? Where is Daniel?
THOMAS 2	He stepped outside the back door to say hello to the children. Am I leaving a trail of my papers?

THOMAS *picks up* NATHAN*'s letter.*

NORA 2   No! Please. Tom.

THOMAS 2   Endless paperwork.

THOMAS keeps a hold of the letter and walks toward the files he left earlier.

I should put this all away in the office. Remember what happened last time the children got a hold of my work? Paper aeroplanes, the lot of it.

NORA 2   No. You can't leave.

She suddenly kisses him very hard. She tries to reach for the letter and fails.

THOMAS 3   Such force. Where did that come from?

NORA 3   I... I... think that is for me?

THOMAS 3   With my name on it?

THOMAS goes to open it. NORA kisses him again. She tries to reach for the letter and fails.

THOMAS 1   Nora.

NORA 1   Put down your work. Put down your work and... let me touch you... let me... show you how good I can make you feel.

NORA kisses THOMAS, again.

THOMAS 1   Alright. Alright I... just let me put this work away.

THOMAS picks up the files. He still has the letter.

NORA 1   No. Just stay with me.

THOMAS 1   Nora.

NORA 1   Come on.

THOMAS 1	Nora.
NORA 1	Just stay with me.
THOMAS 1	Nora! Stop it! You're pissing me off. Just let me put these away with everything else, before the kids fuck up another important document.

THOMAS *leaves*.

NORA 1	And just like that. He walks out the room with the letter in his hand.
NORA 3	And he goes to his desk, places the papers in a drawer and locks it.
NORA 2	And she can barely watch because she doesn't know where he keeps the key.
NORA 3	And she tries to remember a time when she wasn't frightened by his fury.
NORA 1	But she can't, and she is paralysed by panic.
NORA (*all*)	Oh my god.

THOMAS *enters*.

THOMAS 2	Look. Before I sit down to work, I just wanted to say – I'm sorry, I didn't mean to lose my temper, but this time of year is just /
NORA 2	Where do you keep the key for your desk?
THOMAS 2	What? Why? There is nothing in there for /
NORA 2	You never told me, and you should tell me. Please.
THOMAS 2	I don't have time for this nonsense, Nora. I have to work /
NORA (*all*)	No. Stay out of the office.
THOMAS 2	Why? What do you want?

NORA 2	I want us… I want us to be together like it is the last time we will be together.
THOMAS 2	That is a little dramatic.
NORA 1	No, I just want. I want to keep you close.
NORA 3	I want you to be here with me.
NORA 2	Don't step another foot into your office. Because we should… why don't we…
NORA (*all*)	Dance.
NORA 1	Here. I'll put some music on.
NORA 3	We can practise for the party.
NORA 1	Come on! It will be fun!
THOMAS (*all*)	Nora.
NORA 2	Here. I'll put some music on.
NORA 1	We can practise for the party.
NORA 3	Come on! It will be fun!
NORA 2	Just be with me.
NORA 1	Here.
NORA 3	With me.
NORA (*all*)	Like it's the last time.
THOMAS (*all*)	Fine.
NORA (*all*)	So. Dance with me.
	The music begins to play. NORA *takes* THOMAS *in her arms.*
	Right here.
NORA 2	Put your arms there.
NORA 3	Watch my feet.
THOMAS (*all*)	Nora.

They begin to dance.

NORA 1	Right here.
NORA 2	Put your arms there.
NORA 3	Watch my feet.
THOMAS (*all*)	Nora.

The dance gets quicker.

NORA 1	Right here.
NORA 2	Put your arms there.
NORA 3	Watch my feet.
THOMAS (*all*)	Nora. Slower!

And quicker. Finally, THOMAS *drops his hands and backs off.*

Nora!

THOMAS 1	Not so fast. You dance like a wild woman. I can't keep up.
NORA (*all*)	Fine! Then I'll dance with myself if I have to.
THOMAS 1	Fine.
NORA 1	Watch me.

NORA *begins to dance by herself – increasingly violently.* THOMAS *watches. She dances and dances, lost in the moment. There is something wild and free about her movements.* THOMAS *gets lost in the watching. Until* CHRISTINE *enters.*

Christine!

CHRISTINE 1	What a show.
THOMAS 1	Dancing like a madwoman. I swear we haven't had a drink.
NORA 1	Tommy. Promise me, you'll dance with me tomorrow until the end of the night?

THOMAS 1	Do you plan on dancing like that?
NORA 1	Just say you'll dance with me.
THOMAS 1	Sure. Okay… how about a drink? Christine? It's 6 p.m. somewhere.
CHRISTINE 1	Yeah, I'll take a drink of something.
NORA 1	I say we'll drink until dawn – or death – whatever should happen first.
THOMAS 1	You've got a taste for the dramatic today.
	DANIEL *enters*.
DANIEL 1	Those kids are balls of energy. I don't know how you do it.
NORA 1	But you're so good with them.
THOMAS 1	It's true. You'll be a good dad, one day. A drink?
DANIEL 1	I can't think of a reason why not.
THOMAS 1	Nora – bring the kids in, will you? They've spent all afternoon out there, people will think they are feral, and you know how people like to talk.
NORA 1	Okay, I'll get them. Just give me a minute to catch my breath.
	THOMAS *and* DANIEL *leave*.
CHRISTINE 2	Nora. I can't find Nathan. No one is home. Not him. Not his children. But I left him a note asking to speak with him. Maybe, there is still time to fix all this.
NORA 2	I think it would take a miracle.
CHRISTINE 2	In the note, I begged him to think of your children. To think of /
NORA 2	You know what, Christine?

CHRISTINE 2	What?
NORA 2	I wish I could undo my children. I couldn't say it earlier but now I feel free to say anything. I wish they had never been born to me. I wish they had never grown inside of me. I wish this house was empty, as if they had never existed. I wish a doctor had ripped them out of me. A pill had destroyed them before they had ever been destined to be.
	Because they deserve better than me.
CHRISTINE 2	Oh, Nora.
NORA 2	But my life is just a few years too late… nothing at all, really. How different life could have been.
	NORA *steps towards* CHRISTINE. *They look at each other.*
	And I have these feelings. For you. Complicated… feelings. Do you… do you?
CHRISTINE 2	Yes. It's true. I have feelings for you too. Feelings beyond friendship.
NORA 2	But what are we… what are we meant to do with these feelings?
CHRISTINE 2	Well. When we talked earlier you to seemed to warm to the idea that men might cohabit or that /
NORA 2	But isn't it different for men? Everything always seems so different for men.
CHRISTINE 2	But isn't it for once good that we are invisible? That people care less about us? We can hide in plain sight. Plus, the world is changing.
NORA 2	But not quick enough.

CHRISTINE 2	You are choosing to /
NORA 2	What choice does someone like me have?
CHRISTINE 2	But what... what if love... what if I love you.

Silence.

NORA 2	But what if love is not enough?

What if – sometimes – love is not enough.

Silence. THOMAS *enters.*

THOMAS 2	You never said what you wanted to drink, Christine.
CHRISTINE 2	You know – I think I will leave. I'd hate to get in the way.
NORA 2	You aren't in the way.

NORA *reaches out and grabs* CHRISTINE*'s hand.*

Stay.

Silence.

THOMAS 3	Do I need to pour another glass or not?
NORA 3	Please stay.

Silence.

CHRISTINE 3	No. I am afraid, I cannot. Not this lifetime.
THOMAS 3	How many lifetimes do you plan on having, Christine?
CHRISTINE 3	I should hope the next one is rather simpler than this.
THOMAS 3	The world is getting better by the day.
CHRISTINE 3	Maybe for you.
NORA 3	Christine?

CHRISTINE 3   You are at the party tomorrow?

NORA *nods*.

Then... shall I sit with the children while you are out? Then I can see you before and after the party to make sure, I mean... to see you in your dress.

THOMAS 3   What a kind offer, but we could not possibly /

CHRISTINE 3   No. I would like to be here. I did just fix the dress – I would like to see it.

THOMAS 3   Then... we shall see you tomorrow.

CHRISTINE 3   Wonderful. Enjoy your drink.

NORA 3   Thank you. And be careful, it gets dark so early this time of year.

CHRISTINE 3   I think there is still a little light left. And if you should need me, I am only the other side of the river, opposite a statue of... well, of some man who did something.

THOMAS 3   He is actually /

CHRISTINE 3   I shall see you tomorrow.

THOMAS 3   Until tomorrow.

NORA 3   Thank you.

CHRISTINE *leaves*.

THOMAS 3   You know, she reminds me of someone, but I cannot place her... will you come into the kitchen? I thought you could make some hot chocolate for the children. I think they'd like that, would they not?

NORA 3   Yes, I suppose they would.

THOMAS 3   Call them in. And then join us.

THOMAS *leaves*. NORA *goes to the door*.

NORA (*all*)	Children. It's time to come in. It's getting dark.
NORA 1	And as she watches her children run in, for a moment she imagines herself running into the river until her body bashes against the bedrock. Submerging herself. In the cold and calm.
NORA 2	She imagines taking deep breaths of cold water. Rinsing out her ribs until her body becomes bleached and barren.
NORA 3	Washing off the weight and waste of all this life. And there is so much life to live. And the opposite might be a relief. What she realises now, so sharply, so clearly, is that death might be a relief.
THOMAS 2	(*Offstage.*) Songbird?
THOMAS (*all*)	(*Offstage.*) We're waiting.
NORA (*all*)	Your songbird is right here.

DAY THREE

NORA 1	It's dawn and she lies awake. Watching the sun attempting to shine through the curtains.
NORA 2	And she hasn't slept, and she hasn't moved. Pinned in place.
NORA 3	And when she hears her children begin to stir, she exhales for the first time in hours.
NORA 1	She spends the day in a daze. Automated actions of mothering and managing and making sure. A whole lifetime spent – making sure. And from the outside there is no discernible difference to this day in December.
NORA 2	From the outside everything appears to be fine. It's breakfast then lunch then dinner and the children play and laugh and cry and it's a day like any other day.
NORA 3	And suddenly it's 8 p.m., again, and she tucks her children into bed and kisses them on their foreheads. And they smell of sunshine and soap and hope. Her children smell of hope.
NORA 2	And her husband calls her and tells her they must leave. A party is waiting for them. And she kisses each of her children on their foreheads.
NORA 1	And it takes all her strength not to cry. It takes all her strength to stay upright. And she whispers to them.

NORA (*all*)   Goodnight, my sweethearts. I love you.
                      I love you so much, I can barely breathe.

                      The front door creaks open – it's NATHAN.

NATHAN 2   Christine?

CHRISTINE 2   Nathan?

NATHAN 2   They're out?

CHRISTINE 2   Tom and Nora are at a party. I offered to
                      look after their children.

NATHAN 2   You look at home in their living room.

CHRISTINE 2   It's just a living room, like any other. Please
                      come in. Don't stand in the doorway like
                      that. Please.

                      NATHAN *hesitates. Enters.*

NATHAN 2   I got the note you left. I went to where you
                      said you were staying but they said you
                      were here and... it's been a while.

CHRISTINE 2   Years. It's been years.

NATHAN 2   How was his money?

CHRISTINE 2   Don't be like that.

NATHAN 2   Does Nora know about us? Know how we
                      used to be together?

CHRISTINE 2   No. But a lot has changed since then.

NATHAN 2   She doesn't know how you chose a nice
                      house over love?

CHRISTINE 2   It's not that simple.

NATHAN 2   It's not much more complicated. Sometimes
                      I think about how different I might have
                      been if we'd stayed together.... But look...
                      here you are... years after breaking my
                      heart, you're back to take my job.

CHRISTINE 2   I didn't know it was your job. And trust me, my life has not been that simple since we last saw each other. And it's true, Nathan. All those years ago, I left you for a man who had money. I wanted a safe and secure future – something that you couldn't provide.

NATHAN 2   Then why aren't you still with him?

CHRISTINE 2   Because the world has changed and back then I didn't know what I really wanted. I thought I had no choice back then.

NATHAN 2   There is always a choice.

CHRISTINE 2   No, there isn't.

NATHAN 2   So. What do you want? Are you about to propose a second chance? A rekindling? Because I don't think now is the time for romance.

CHRISTINE 2   No. I am not proposing a romance. There is a lot to tell you but there isn't time… I know what you have done, what you've done to Nora. But despite that I still care for you. And so, I suppose what I am proposing is that you are not this man. This blackmailing, mean, malicious man.

NATHAN 2   Maybe I have become that man.

CHRISTINE 2   No. I know you. I know you so well, Nathan McKinnon. The years do not change that you are a good man who has faced difficult times.

NATHAN 2   Difficult times? I am broken, Christine. My heart, my everything is smashed to pieces. And I thought it was mended by meeting my wife but it seems there are a thousand ways for a person to break.

CHRISTINE 2   I understand that you miss having someone.

NATHAN 2	No. I don't miss it. I crave it.
CHRISTINE 2	Then let me help you.
NATHAN 2	But Christine…
CHRISTINE 2	Maybe the two of us – shipwrecked survivors – can find a way. To be friends, maybe. I am not talking romance, you understand but… Please. Be the man better than what has happened to him.
	CHRISTINE *reaches out and holds* NATHAN. NATHAN *is reluctant but finally gives way to the warmth of her arms.*
NATHAN 2	It has been years since I have been held.
CHRISTINE (*all*)	I know.
NATHAN 2	You are softening me to help your friend.
CHRISTINE 2	Or maybe I simply see another friend who I hurt, many years ago. Who I wish to help heal.
NATHAN 2	But I've done terrible things. Unforgivable things.
CHRISTINE (*all*)	I know.
NATHAN 2	Then why are you being so kind to me? It's been years since…
CHRISTINE 2	Shouldn't people look after one another during terrible times like this? Nathan McKinnon – you can choose to be a good man.
CHRISTINE 1	Please, Nathan. Don't do this. This isn't you.
CHRISTINE 3	As you said yourself – there is always a choice.
NATHAN 3	But, Christine… I cannot undo what I have done. There is no way for me to take back the letter.

CHRISTINE 1   Then maybe we should just let them read it.
Because if it's love… well, that has to mean
something. Doesn't it?

NATHAN 1   I've no idea.

I'm sorry… for the things I've done.

CHRISTINE 3   I am too. It seems we have both lived a
million lives and I would like to try and
help you. We can meet? When all this has
passed? Take the time to see the truth in
each other.

NATHAN 3   Yes. I would like that. And thank you.

CHRISTINE (*all*)   For what?

NATHAN 2   You helped me feel less alone. Which is the
greatest gift.

Silence.

CHRISTINE 2   I think I hear people outside. Quickly out
the back, just in case. Goodnight, Nathan.

NATHAN 2   Goodnight, Christine… and… goodnight.

NATHAN *slips out the back door. We hear
voices outside.* NORA *and* THOMAS
*return to the sitting room. Taking off their
jackets – they haven't noticed* CHRISTINE.

THOMAS 1   Nora! Won't you stop this?

NORA 1   But I wasn't finished dancing!

THOMAS 1   I think you've danced quite enough.

NORA 1   All I wanted was one last dance. One last
dance.

NORA *suddenly spots* CHRISTINE *in the
corner of the room.*

Christine.

CHRISTINE 1	You had a good night?
THOMAS 1	The best. How were the kids?
CHRISTINE 1	They've just been sleeping since you left. You look great, Nora.
THOMAS 1	Isn't she the prettiest thing you've ever seen? Beautiful. Stubborn too. Her pretty little heart is stubborn.
NORA 1	You should have let me dance longer.
THOMAS 1	You made quite an exit, I had to drag you away from dancing. During which I've worked up a thirst and I need a nightcap.
NORA 1	And I'll have one!
THOMAS 1	A whisky? More like water for you, Nora Helmer.

THOMAS *exits.*

CHRISTINE 1	I spoke to Nathan.
NORA 1	And?
CHRISTINE 1	He won't bother you again. I promise.
NORA 1	But Tommy still has that letter locked away and I'm still... fucked.
CHRISTINE 1	What if you told him what you did?
NORA 1	Why?
CHRISTINE 1	I know it will be hard but – do you want to live with all these lies?
NORA 1	But it will destroy him.
CHRISTINE 1	But if he loves you, Nora. He has to understand, what you did, you did for love.

THOMAS *walks in, interrupting the moment.*

THOMAS 1   I love this time of year. It feels like you are just given constant reasons to drink.

CHRISTINE 1   I should go. Goodnight, Nora.

NORA 1   Goodnight, Christine.

THOMAS 1   And a merry Christmas!

                CHRISTINE takes one last look at NORA.

CHRISTINE 1   Merry Christmas.

                She leaves.

THOMAS 2   You look tired.

NORA 2   I am tired.

                Silence.

                Stop looking at me like that.

THOMAS 2   I can look at my little prize however I'd like to.

NORA 2   Don't say that.

THOMAS 2   It is just... you are the most beautiful thing.

NORA 2   You barely spoke to me all night.

THOMAS 2   Because I like to watch you. I like to pretend you are my secret. I like to pretend that I am taking you home for the first time. That I will be alone with you for the first time. And you're standing there – beautiful and trembling.

                THOMAS moves towards NORA.

NORA 2   What is beautiful about a woman trembling?

THOMAS 2   Trembling with lust – not trepidation.

                He starts to kiss her neck.

NORA 2   How can you tell the difference?

THOMAS *puts his hand on her leg, moves it up her thigh.*

Tom.

THOMAS 2	I cannot bear to take my lips off your skin.
NORA 2	Tom.
THOMAS 2	Can you feel how much I want you?

THOMAS *places her hand on his groin. She snaps it away.*

NORA 2	I'm not in the mood.
THOMAS 2	But I'm your husband.
NORA 2	And I'm your wife and I'm not in the mood.
THOMAS 2	I have always managed to get you in the mood once we've started.

THOMAS *grabs at her clothes.*

NORA 2	Stop it. You're drunk.
THOMAS 2	I'd like to see some of that skin…
NORA 2	Stop it.
THOMAS 2	Come here!

A knock at the door. THOMAS *drops his hands.*

Oh, what now.

NORA *opens the door to* DANIEL. *He enters.*

NORA 3	Daniel.
DANIEL 3	Hello, dear Helmers.
THOMAS 3	It's not like you to call at night.
DANIEL 3	I am not interrupting, am I? I saw your light was on and /

NORA 3	I am quite glad you are here.
DANIEL 3	You both looked so happy tonight and here you are in your happy home.
THOMAS 3	You looked rather happy yourself tonight.
DANIEL 3	And why wouldn't I? Why shouldn't one make the most of this world? As much as one can, and for as long as one can... also the wine was excellent.
THOMAS 3	I hope my head does not regret it tomorrow.
DANIEL 3	You never get anything in this life without paying for it.
NORA 3	That is the truth.
THOMAS 3	And what would you know about paying for anything? Silly girl. A drink? Daniel? My skylark can fetch you one?
DANIEL 3	No, no. I shall simply ask what I came for – a cigar. I have left mine at home and I wished to enjoy one on my walk. There is nothing quite like smoking while it is snowing.
NORA 3	But is it wise for you to smoke? When... you have been feeling so tired.
THOMAS 3	A man can do as he wishes, Nora. And of course, my friend. Anything.
	THOMAS *gets a cigar and cuts it.*
NORA 3	How are you feeling?
DANIEL 3	You know, I am thinking of taking a trip. I am finding this bad weather rather relentless, time for a change, maybe.
NORA 3	But I will miss you. Ever such a lot.
DANIEL 3	And I will miss you. Ever such a lot.

THOMAS 3	Do not forget some matches, here take mine.
	THOMAS *hands a cigar and a box of matches to* DANIEL.
DANIEL 3	Thank you.
THOMAS 3	Goodnight. Enjoy the snow.
NORA 3	Wrap up warm, Daniel. It is going to be a cold night.
DANIEL 3	Goodnight. Thank you for the light. Such light.
	DANIEL *leaves*.
THOMAS 1	He has been drinking. It makes him so, far away.
NORA 1	And he will only get further away.
THOMAS 1	It's a little late for riddles.
NORA 1	He is ill. Really ill.
THOMAS 1	What?
NORA 1	Cancer. Tommy.
THOMAS 1	What? I should go and /
NORA 1	No. He wanted me to keep it a secret, but tonight I don't believe in secrets, any more.
THOMAS 1	Why didn't he tell me? Lie to me like this.
NORA 1	Because he wants your friendship to be – happy. And sometimes, there is a difference between happiness and truth.
THOMAS 3	Such news... come here. Come here.
	THOMAS *suddenly grabs* NORA.
	I never want to let go of you. The thought of losing you my songbird... is too much. The thought that I would let a delicate creature

like you, be hurt. I mean after one evening
of drinking wine and you are already
unsteady. I shall protect us both, from
anything, everything.

NORA 3   I am not unsteady.

THOMAS 3   Oh. I know you better than you know
yourself. I know what is best for you. My
prized possession. My lovely little skylark.

NORA *pushes him away.*

Nora, please. I am vowing to protect you.

NORA 2   Am I just a little ornamental bird to you?
Just a possession?

THOMAS 2   It's just a word.

NORA 2   Words can be powerful.

THOMAS 2   Oh, please. What would you know about the
power of words?

Silence.

NORA 2   There was a letter, one you locked away
with your files. I suddenly thought it could
be something urgent.

THOMAS 2   It can wait until the morning.

NORA 2   No. I don't think it can.

THOMAS 2   There is no such thing as urgent at
Christmas.

NORA 2   Then a gift. Maybe? A little Christmas gift.
I'd hate to miss something pretty to put on
the mantelpiece. Please. For me. For silly
old me.

THOMAS 2   Fine. I shall go hunt it out.

NORA 2   Thank you.

THOMAS 2	You really are very ridiculous.
NORA 2	Oh, I know. I am utterly ridiculous.
	THOMAS *kisses her on the forehead and leaves.* NORA *is left.*
NORA 3	My skeleton.
NORA 1	My ribcage.
NORA 2	My heart.
NORA 3	Blood and bile and body and /
NORA 2	Polluted and poisoned /
NORA 1	From milk into madness.
NORA 3	There is just so much life to live.
NORA (*all*)	Too much.
NORA 2	Must silence these thoughts.
NORA 1	Must drown it out.
NORA 3	Flood it out.
NORA 1	Must silence these thoughts.
NORA 3	Must drown it out.
NORA 2	Flood it out.
NORA 3	Must silence these thoughts.
NORA 2	Must drown it out.
NORA 1	Flood it out.
NORA 3	I'll run into the river.
NORA 2	Until I brush up against the bedrock.
NORA 1	And I breathe only cold water.
NORA (*all*)	I'll drown myself.
NORA 1	Goodbye. My sweethearts.
NORA 2	Goodbye.

NORA 3	Goodbye.
NORA 1	Goodbye. Goodbye. Goodbye. Goodbye. Good.... good.

NORA *takes a deep breath, turns to leave.* THOMAS *walks in clutching* NATHAN'*s letter.*

THOMAS 1	What the fuck is this? Nora? This letter? Is this true? What you, how you got that money? Is this true?

NORA *nods.*

What?

NORA 1	Yes. It's true.
THOMAS 1	And do you know who sent it? Who sent this letter? Who... oh my god.
NORA 1	I was trying to save you.
THOMAS 1	Save me? This is your way of saving me? By lying to me? About all this. All this borrowed money. You said it was your dad's but you... it was illegal what you... Nora. What the fuck were you thinking? If anyone else found out – it's illegal, Nora. This is police, this is prison, what the fuck were you thinking? And the kids? I left you to look after my kids and... and we don't have fucking anything and still you managed to fuck it up more. You fucked everything up, you stupid little bitch. Because who else knows? Who else, look at me. Fucking looking at me. I said who else knows?

THOMAS *goes to grab* NORA, *but she keeps moving away.*

Look at me. I said look at me. I said look at me. I said look at me.

THOMAS *grabs on to* NORA, *lifts his hand to backhand her. The sudden cry of a child from another room. It stops* THOMAS *instantly, he lets go of her. Drops his hand.*

NORA 1   I should /

THOMAS 1   No. Stay here.

                  She'll settle.

                  The crying stops. A long silence.

                  Why, Nora. Why did you /

NORA 1   When you got sick and you weren't earning,
                  I had to find a way to pay for everything,
                  because otherwise we would have lost it.
                  We were on the edge of losing everything
                  and I brought us back. I did that. And I did
                  it for love. I risked it all for... love.

THOMAS 1   Why didn't you just tell me?

NORA 1   Because I was scared.

NORA 2   I was scared of you.

NORA 3   Because I am scared of everything.

                  Long silence.

NORA 1   And his mobile beeps with a message.

NORA 2   The house phone rings.

NORA 3   A telegram delivered.

THOMAS 1   Oh, what now.

                  THOMAS *goes to receive the message.*

NORA 1   Silence and stillness surrounds and drowns
                  her.

NORA 3   To think of waves.

NORA 2   And wounds.

NORA 1	And washing away.
	For the first time the NORAS *suddenly acknowledge each other.*
NORA (*all*)	This is it.
NORA 2	This is really it.
NORA 1	I'm sorry.
NORA 3	But maybe there was never any choice.
NORA 2	Maybe this really is everything.
NORA 1	But I...
NORA 3	I know. I know.
	Silence. THOMAS *enters. The* NORAS *become unnoticeable to each other again.*
NORA 2	What was it?
	THOMAS *hesitates.*
THOMAS 2	Nathan. It was Nathan McKinnon... He was the one who was going to blackmail you?
NORA 2	What did he say?
THOMAS 2	That he will no longer notify the police or anyone of any wrongdoing. If we quietly pay back your debt he will destroy any evidence of any wrongdoing.
	He will destroy... we are free.
NORA 2	But how? Why?
THOMAS 2	He said he wished to be a better man. He said...
	Silence.
	We are free.
NORA (*all*)	I am free.

THOMAS 2   And I am saved. We are both... saved.

             THOMAS *goes to her, she moves away.*

             I am sorry for what I said... I was angry.
             I'm sorry for... oh, my skylark. This must
             have worried you.

             You made a silly decision because you didn't
             know any better. I forgive you for what you
             did, and I am sorry for my angry words, but
             you must understand... I thought our world
             was crumbling around us. But now, I see
             what you did was for love. I forgive you.

NORA 2   It's amazing how quickly...

             NORA *turns to leave.*

THOMAS 2   What? Where are you going?

NORA 2   To change.

             NORA *steps in the room next door to get
             changed.*

THOMAS 2   Yes, you're right. Now is the time for calm.
             You must have been so frightened little
             songbird but don't worry... I shall make
             sure no harm is ever done to you. It will take
             time, Nora. To forget all this but tomorrow
             will be quite different. Do you ever think
             I could bring myself to disown you – no, to
             forgive you frees my heart. I have given you
             the gift of a second chance and that brings
             me joy. If you think about it, for the second
             time – it seems – I have made you a wife
             and a mother. Never be frightened again.
             Little songbird. Never again.

             NORA *walks in. Dressed in her normal
             daytime clothes.*

THOMAS 3   You have changed?

NORA 3	I have changed.
THOMAS 3	You would be better to change into your nightclothes. Soon it will be time for some quiet.
NORA 3	I do not have time for quiet. When there is such a lot to say to you.
THOMAS 3	I do not understand.
NORA 3	No, it is I who has not understood you. Until this very evening. We have been married for years and does it not occur to you that this is the first time we have had a serious conversation?
THOMAS 3	Nonsense.
NORA 3	Exactly. We have spoken nothing but nonsense for all these years.
	You see you never understood me. First Father and now you.
THOMAS 3	Two men who loved you?
NORA 3	Two men who thought it fun to love me. I look back on it all and I realise everything is arranged the way you want it. I simply took over your taste or I pretended I did – I don't really know which. Now, I see I have actually been living as a pauper, from hand to mouth. I perform tricks for you and you gave me money and food because that is all you wanted from me. Maybe it is your fault that I have done nothing with my life? Or maybe it was Father's or maybe… or maybe it is my own.
THOMAS 3	You have not been happy?
NORA 3	I used to think I was… but what I see now is our home has been nothing but a playroom. I am a doll-wife.

THOMAS 3	Maybe, there is some truth in what you say. But, now you can learn to be another way.
NORA 3	Learn? You are trying to educate me in being a wife? How about teaching me to be a mother? You did say just moments ago that I was not fit to be a mother.
THOMAS 3	In a moment of crisis.
NORA 3	But the truth is – you are right. I am not fit to be with the children. If I am to learn to be a mother, first I must learn to be myself... by myself.
THOMAS 3	What?
NORA 3	I am leaving you.
THOMAS 3	You have lost your mind.
NORA 3	No. For the first time this lifetime I see it so clearly. I see it so clearly it would scare you.
THOMAS 3	I am scared, Nora. What you are saying...
NORA 3	I will take nothing but what is mine.
	NORA *looks around the room.*
	Which seems to be nothing at all.
THOMAS 3	Leave your husband? Your children? What will people say?
NORA 3	I cannot help what people will say.
THOMAS 3	It is monstrous for you to leave your children. Your most sacred duty.
NORA 3	A sacred duty? I have a duty equally sacred – a duty to myself.
THOMAS 3	First and foremost, you are a mother and a wife.
NORA 2	No.

NORA 1	No.
NORA 3	No.
	I believe that I am first and foremost a human being.
NORA (*all*)	Because my heart beats for me.
NORA 2	And not once have you asked for my opinion about our life together.
NORA 1	You've hurt me. You've done terrible things.
THOMAS 1	I am sorry if I have hurt you. I am so very... but if you walk – you'll have nothing. Nora. Your purse is empty. You have no idea of how the world works.
NORA (*all*)	Then I'd like to learn.
THOMAS 3	You don't love me?
	When did you stop?
NORA 1	This evening.
NORA (*all*)	I was waiting for a miracle.
NORA 1	I thought you might stand up for me.
NORA 3	I was waiting for you to see what this marriage really is and to take equal blame for it.
THOMAS 2	I would gladly work day and night for you, endure sorrow and hardship for your sake. But no man can be expected to sacrifice /
NORA 2	His honour? His pride? No, this man would not sacrifice it. When every day, thousands of women sacrifice their honour for men.
THOMAS 3	You think and talk like a child.
NORA 3	Maybe. But you think and talk like a man I have no interest in sharing my life with.

NORA 1	Take a look around. Is this what you want for us? For life? Take a fucking look around?
THOMAS (*all*)	But the children?
	Silence.
NORA 3	For the last few days I have done nothing but send the children outside to play. Employ a nanny, then they will have an adult who actually spends time with them.
NORA 2	There is so much about myself and my desires that I do not understand but wish to… and I won't subject the children to that. Their world is not ready for mine.
NORA 1	The kids' uniforms need washed before they go back to school after Christmas. Iron them too, won't you? I like them to look smart. The iron is kept under the sink. The steam setting is broken but… you'll make do. Just like I did.
THOMAS 1	But you are walking out of this house with nothing. No money. No family. You've no one but me. There is nowhere else for you. You'll freeze to death.
NORA 3	I will leave your ring.
NORA 2	I'll leave my keys.
NORA 1	I'll leave my phone… in it you'll find all the dates you'll need for all the kids' appointments and… look after them, won't you?
THOMAS 3	But where will you go?
NORA 3	You know, Thomas. I have never seen beyond this street, not in years. So, I think I will walk there and simply keep on

walking because I want to see… I just want to see what could happen.

THOMAS 1   But you've got no friends. No family. No money. Bus stop around the corner… that's all you've got. So. Don't be stupid.

NORA 1   Oh, fuck me, do I feel stupid. I feel stupid for staying so fucking long. Because I think I hate you. I think I might actually hate you.

NORA 2   I love life. Thomas. I love life so much I could burst, and you took that from me. And how dare you take it. Because my life is not ridiculous. My life is worth something.

NORA 3   For weeks we have been raising toasts to the war ending, but it seems not all wars have ended, not all wars have battlefields.

THOMAS 3   This is not a war.

NORA 3   Then why are we both so wounded?

THOMAS 1   Nora? Please. I can change.

NORA 1   Then change.

NORA *walks out the front door. The door closes.* THOMAS *disappears.*

NORA 3   And it's 1918. And she walks through the snow, quicker and quicker until she is almost running, until her face flushes red with the exertion, until she can't tell the difference between her tears and sweat. She runs until her front door is nothing but a dot.

NORA 2   And it's 1968. And she walks through the snow until she ends up on the doorstep where her friend is staying. She holds her heart and hope in her hands as her knuckles knock the door. Her friend answers it in her nightdress and tears fill her eyes.

NORA 1	And it's 2018. And she walks through the snow until she reaches that bus stop, the one place she can shelter. And she stands under it, for the longest moments of her life. Tears dripping down her face, freezing as they fall. And she realises she has nowhere else to go.
NORA (*all*)	And tears fall down her face.
NORA 3	And she runs, and she runs, and she runs. Until she falls to the ground in exhilaration and exhaustion.
NORA 2	And she asks if she can stay the night. And she steps into her friend's home and into her arms that hold her.
NORA 1	And she knows there are no shelters near here. No community centres. No nothing. Not any more.
NORA (*all*)	And tears fall down her face.
NORA 3	And as she lays down in the snow, she knows that she would give up a lifetime of imprisonment, for fifteen minutes of free. And she lets the cold and the snow hold her like a hug, and she smiles, and she closes her eyes.
NORA 2	And as they close the front door, one hand slips into another. Neither of them thinks about anything else but the feeling of skin on skin. Two women, terrified, electrified by the possibility of this new existence.
NORA 1	And in the distance, she watches her husband walk towards her. Shaking and in shock, she knows that somehow, someway, someday, she'll be free.
NORA 3	It will be okay.

NORA 1	One day. Everything will be okay.
NORA 2	We can get through this. We always do.
NORA 1	Because what if this isn't everything.
NORA 2	What if this is just the beginning.
NORA 3	Because we won't stop.
NORA 2	We will never stop.
NORA 2	And I'm sorry we weren't quick enough.
NORA 1	To save you.
NORA 2	To help you save yourself.
NORA 3	Because I love you.
NORA 1	Because we are angry.
NORA 2	We are fucking furious.
NORA 3	And we are coming for your daughters, your sisters, your mothers, your lovers.
NORA 2	And we won't stop.
NORA 1	We'll never stop.
NORA 3	Until there is nothing left to do.
NORA 1	A woman.
NORA 2	A woman.
NORA 3	A woman walks /
NORA 1	A woman walks out of her home and she just...

The End.

'A great published script makes you understand what the play is, at its heart' *Slate Magazine*

Enjoyed this book? Choose from hundreds more classic and contemporary plays from Nick Hern Books, the UK's leading independent theatre publisher.

Our full range is available to browse online now, including:

Award-winning plays from leading contemporary dramatists, including *King Charles III* by Mike Bartlett, *Anne Boleyn* by Howard Brenton, *Jerusalem* by Jez Butterworth, *A Breakfast of Eels* by Robert Holman, *Chimerica* by Lucy Kirkwood, *The Night Alive* by Conor McPherson, *The James Plays* by Rona Munro, *Nell Gwynn* by Jessica Swale, and many more…

Ground-breaking drama from the most exciting up-and-coming playwrights, including Vivienne Franzmann, James Fritz, Ella Hickson, Anna Jordan, Jack Thorne, Phoebe Waller-Bridge, Tom Wells, and many more…

Twentieth-century classics, including *Cloud Nine* by Caryl Churchill, *Death and the Maiden* by Ariel Dorfman, *Pentecost* by David Edgar, *Angels in America* by Tony Kushner, *Long Day's Journey into Night* by Eugene O'Neill, *The Deep Blue Sea* by Terence Rattigan, *Machinal* by Sophie Treadwell, and many more…

Timeless masterpieces from playwrights throughout the ages, including Anton Chekhov, Euripides, Henrik Ibsen, Federico García Lorca, Christopher Marlowe, Molière, William Shakespeare, Richard Brinsley Sheridan, Oscar Wilde, and many more…

Every playscript is a world waiting to be explored. Find yours at **www.nickhernbooks.co.uk** – you'll receive a 20% discount, plus free UK postage & packaging for orders over £30.

'Publishing plays gives permanent form to an evanescent art, and allows many more people to have some kind of experience of a play than could ever see it in the theatre' *Nick Hern, publisher*

www.nickhernbooks.co.uk

A Nick Hern Book

Nora : A Doll's House first published as a paperback original in Great Britain in 2019 by Nick Hern Books Limited, The Glasshouse, 49a Goldhawk Road, London W12 8QP, in association with the Citizens Theatre, Glasgow

Nora : A Doll's House copyright © 2019 Stef Smith

Stef Smith has asserted her right to be identified as the author of this work

Cover photograph by Mihaela Bodlovic

Designed and typeset by Nick Hern Books, London
Printed in the UK by Mimeo Ltd, Huntingdon, Cambridgeshire PE29 6XX

A CIP catalogue record for this book is available from the British Library

ISBN 978 1 84842 844 7